CHOSEN

TO BE A

DISCIPLE

WHAT EVERY PERSON SHOULD KNOW

Robert J. Charles, PhD, DMin

To my loving wife, Gina

To all the laypeople, elders, pastors, administrators, theology students, and professors
that I've met through the years who would like to be disciples of Jesus...

This book is for you.

He chose us in Him before the foundation of the world,
that we should be holy and without blame before Him in love.
—Ephesians 1:4 (NKJV)

You did not choose Me, but I chose you and appointed you
that you should go and bear fruit, and that your fruit should remain,
that whatever you ask the Father in My name He may give you.
—John 15:16 (NKJV)

But we are bound to give thanks to God always for you, brethren beloved by the Lord,
because God from the beginning chose you for salvation
through sanctification by the Spirit and belief in the truth.
—2 Thessalonians 2:13 (NKJV)

CONTENTS

YOUR FREE GIFT

Download Your FREE 30 BIBLICAL PROMISES TO OVERCOME ANY CHALLENGE

Click https://go.robertjcharles.com/30BiblicalPromises

At some point, everyone on this earth faces a tough challenge.

Help is on the way!

God has your back. His Word will empower you to face any trial or tribulation.

May these 30 promises from God give you the strength and the resilience you need to move forward.

To get your FREE 30 BIBLICAL PROMISES
TO OVERCOME ANY CHALLENGE,
Click on this link https://go.robertjcharles.com/30BiblicalPromises

PREFACE

————⟨◆—◆—◆⟩————

I'm always concerned about the fact that many people leave our churches every year. In February 2019, after attending the NAD (North American Division) Church Plant Boot Camp in Florida and reading some books, my soul was rekindled with the need for church members to be disciples of Jesus. Discipleship became the motto of a school of evangelism that we have for some churches in the Greater New York Conferences, where I presented two seminars on discipleship. I became more and more concerned about the status quo of some churches.

In July 2019, I was in Mexico, studying for a PhD in Business Administration. Dr. Emmer Chacon gave an assignment for his class, Biblical Worldview II. We were required to do some research and prepare a paper on a theological topic. I thought that was a good place to write about discipleship. While I was researching for the task, God convinced me that I must write a book on this topic. And to prove that this was what I needed to do, the Lord worked many incredible miracles throughout the process of producing this book.

In this post-COVD-19 era, if you are still alive, there's a reason for it. God has a purpose for you. He wants you to become a disciple of Jesus. Megatrends will continue to change and reshape our world with disruptive innovation at an unprecedented pace. More than ever, it is critical for you to focus on that which remains constant: God's purpose for your life, to be a disciple.

I invite you to read this book with a spirit of prayer so that the Holy Spirit can reveal to you the truth found within these pages for a deeper spiritual experience. My hope for you is that after reading this book, you will discover the necessity and the joy of being a disciple of Jesus. It's so fulfilling and so enjoyable to be in fellowship with Jesus.

PART I

WHY BE A DISCIPLE?

CHAPTER 1

——◆—◆—◆——

CHOSEN TO UNDERSTAND THE NECESSITY OF BEING A DISCIPLE

"Discipleship, at heart, involves transformation at the deepest levels of our understanding, affection, and will by the Holy Spirit, through the Word of God, and in relationship with the people of God."

—Jim Putman

From 1965 to 2017, the Seventh-day Adventist Church grew to 37,138,884 members. Of these, 14,521,088 chose to leave—a net loss of 42 percent. "In effect, four of every ten church members are slipping away."[1] In the vast majority of denominations, churches are declining or at a plateau.

It is heartbreaking to see that, after 15 or 25 years, some churches are declining or remain with the same level of membership. Something is wrong. It does not need to be that way. One of the reasons could be that many church members do not understand how to be disciples of Jesus. That is a real tragedy!

In this world, there is real controversy. This fight must concern each of us on this planet; everyone needs to understand the effect of the issue.

> Within the domain of every human heart, this controversy is repeated.

American Christian pioneer Ellen Gould White[2] writes, "Many look at this conflict between Christ and Satan as having no special bearing on their own life; for them, it has little interest. However, within the domain of every human heart, this controversy is repeated."[3]

We are all in a battle. We all have our fights. To win this battle and restore in our souls the image of God, Jesus gave to His followers a precise order: *make disciples*. Before Jesus left His disciples, He commanded them to go and make disciples of all the nations. This order is known as the Great Commission. It is so important that we find it at the end of each of the four Gospels: Matthew 28:18–20, Mark 16:15–20, Luke 24:45–49, and John 20:21–23. But the Great Commission is more than adding people to a new church. It is God's way of helping men and women to become more like Jesus. That is why the enemy will do all in his power to prevent the church from accomplishing this very task. The Great Commission—making disciples—is Jesus's last will for His church.

The Problem

I would like you to acknowledge that there is a problem. Something is being terribly neglected in our process of evangelism. This is very serious and can influence you to live a shallow Christian life.

Joi Tyrrell, communication director for the Bermuda Conference, thinks that the significant number of members leaving the church is "a cause of great concern" and "the problem facing the church today."[4]

Although discipleship, in Jesus's words, is the strategy of winning the world, for Opoku Onyinah (2017), this order has been grossly ignored and replaced with the making of converts. Mark Brown (2012) identifies the problem as the fact that the church is teaching people how to become Christians, but not how to become disciples.

Bill Hull (2006) has argued that the church is creating a non-discipleship Christianity. Church culture in the global North—along with Australia, New Zealand, and South Africa—has broadly accepted the idea of non-discipleship Christianity. People can be Christians without making any effort to submit to and follow Christ.

Hull affirms, "How the church has missed this obvious mandate can only be attributed to a diabolical scheme. The crisis at the heart of the church is that we give disciple making lip service, but do not practice it. We have lost the integrity of our mission."[5]

Alejandro Bullón (2017) affirms that the problem is that most Christians are content with being believers. They are not disciple-

> How the church has missed this obvious mandate can only be attributed to a diabolical scheme. The crisis at the heart of the church is that we give disciple making lip service, but do not practice it. We have lost the integrity of our mission.

makers; they are mere spectators of the Sabbath program. They judge and evaluate the program, approve or disapprove. They contribute their tithes and offerings but are not committed to the mission.

Dallas Willard (2006) writes that "the governing assumption today, among professing Christians, is that we can be 'Christians' forever and never become disciples. That is the standard teaching now—the 'Great Omission' from the Great Commission."

Jeffrey Lynn (2014) adds another dimension to the problem. Many churches have their focus on evangelism at the expense of discipleship. They seek mostly to win converts and do not facilitate the process by which converts become disciples. Many have missed this point: Matthew 28:19–20 is all about making disciples, not winning converts. As G. Earl Knight writes, "An emphasis on discipleship and not just membership will prove to be effective in caring for the members."[6]

> Most evangelism today is obsessed with getting someone to make a decision; the apostles, however, were obsessed with making disciples.

Similarly, Scot McKnight argues, "Most evangelism today is obsessed with getting someone to make a decision; the apostles, however, were obsessed with making disciples."[7]

When we consider the history of God's people, we can see how easy it was for us to shift from His will. Reread the history of Israel. Look at the early church. These early Christians wanted to stay at Jerusalem, despite Jesus's order to go from Jerusalem to "all Judea and Samaria, and to the end of the earth" (Acts 1:8 NKJV). White has said, "When the disciples followed their inclination to remain in large numbers in Jerusalem, persecution was permitted to come upon them, and they were scattered to all parts of the inhabited world."[8]

The command to make disciples is evident in the Bible, but many Christians today are far from understanding and following this order. In the past, the disciples did not adhere to the instructions of Jesus. After His ascension, they stayed at Jerusalem, contrary to Jesus's command. It took the fire of persecution for them to leave Jerusalem and spread the good news in other countries.

> The same way the first disciples misunderstood the command not to station only in Jerusalem, many Christians today do not understand the order of Jesus to be a disciple and to make disciples.

The same way the first disciples misunderstood the command not to station only in Jerusalem, many Christians today do not understand the order of Jesus to be a disciple and to make disciples. I pray to God that we open our minds to understand the problem that we are facing today regarding the Great Commission. Even though we are sincere Christians, human hearts do not always follow the full will of God entirely. For three years, Jesus had to redirect the disciples from time to time regarding their misunderstandings of His teaching. Our only hope is to be in continuous fellowship with Jesus. He will transform us and guide us all the way.

John Thomas Green (2012) argues that the command to make disciples is imperative for Christians to follow. The North American church has struggled in this endeavor. While churches are doing great in programs and ministries, these programs and departments are not adequately making disciples of Jesus Christ. Lynn (2014), referring to George Barna's research, states that "the current state of making disciples of Jesus Christ … is dismal." Lynn indicates that in most local churches, we can find systems for evangelism, but we do not have any systems in place with a specific goal of discipleship. Over the course of many years, churches have developed an evangelistic culture.

"Bar-code Christians"— people who believe the right things but don't follow Jesus.

In his 2006 book on discipleship, *The Complete Book of Discipleship: On Being and Making Followers of Christ,* Hull refers to "bar-code Christians"— people who believe the right things but don't follow Jesus. In *Disciple-Making Pastor,* his book published in 2007, Hull affirms that multiplication is critical to reach the world and fulfill the Great Commission:

The Great Commission without multiplication is evangelism paralyzed from the neck down. By specifically commanding the making of disciples, Jesus specified the work product of the church. He did not say, "Make converts" or "Make Christians."[9]

The Great Commission without multiplication is evangelism paralyzed from the neck down.

White has said, "The true missionary spirit has deserted the churches that make so exalted a profession; their hearts are no longer aglow with love for souls, and a desire to lead them into the fold of Christ."[10] Strength comes through exercise, White adds: "Thus, the Christian who will not exercise his God-given powers not only fails to grow up into Christ, but he loses the strength he already had; he becomes a spiritual paralytic."[11]

> Strength comes through exercise, White adds: "Thus, the Christian who will not exercise his God-given powers not only fails to grow up into Christ, but he loses the strength he already had; he becomes a spiritual paralytic."

You must address this situation in your life on a personal level. God wants you to be a disciple. I say to not only be a believer, but a *disciple*. If you do not, you will lose the most exceptional opportunity of your life.

The Consequence

This situation has severe consequences on many lives and on the local churches.

Lynn (2014) has said that in our generation, the crisis of the church is a crisis of *product*. What kind of believer does the church produce? Church members or disciples? The outcome expected by Jesus is that the church will produce disciples. Christ ordered His church to "make disciples" (Matthew 28:19 NKJV).

Many Christians neither understand nor follow the order of Jesus to make disciples. That's why some believers are weak and do not experience the joy of salvation. They are ready to leave the church over any problem that arises. They lose their joy—or what should be joy to a child of God. Or sometimes they stay in the church, but their presence makes it hard to distinguish between those who believe in Jesus and those who do not.

Cole (2018) mentions that the church in America in many ways reflects the culture of America. American culture encourages receiving over giving. The average church member may be inclined to view the church from a consumer mentality rather than a serving and giving mindset. Church members are tempted to desire being served rather than serving.

Bobby William Harrington (2017) quotes Dallas Willard to say that the most significant issue in the world today is identifying believers who "will become disciples—students, apprentices, practitioners—of Jesus Christ, steadily learning from Him."

Roxburgh and Romanuk (2006) declare that consumerist views of faith encourage churches to develop an overprogrammed church culture. Consumerism exists as an often-unchallenged assumption in American life, especially in churches.

Vanessa Marie Seifert (2013) indicates that consumers look for what is appealing, and the attractive church model caters to this consumerist church perspective.

Cole (2018) adds that this consumer mentality naturally spreads into the church. Ministry slowly shifts from serving to being served.

White writes, "Many have a form of godliness, their names are upon the church records, but they have a spotted record in heaven."[12] She adds, "Today a large part of those who compose our congregations are dead in trespasses and sins. They come and go like the door upon its hinges. For years they have complacently listened to the most solemn, soul-stirring truths, but they have not put them in practice. Therefore, they are less and less sensible of the preciousness of truth."[13] She writes, "Many there are against whose names will be found written in the books of heaven, not producers, but consumers."[14] She indicates the danger of this consumerist culture and of "those who do little or nothing themselves for Christ."[15]

Bullón (2017) argues, "We have many members but few disciples. Don't you think it's time we made a change?"

The Importance of Being a Disciple

One of the solutions to the issue of plateauing or declining churches is to refocus and embrace the order of Jesus again by making disciples. When Jesus chooses someone, He calls this person to fullness of life. But this can be possible only through the discipleship process.

Onyinah (2017) writes that due to the importance of discipleship, the whole Godhead—the Father, the Son, and the Holy Spirit—is involved in the commission that Jesus gives to His disciples. In the Great Commission, Jesus said, "All authority in heaven and on earth has been given to me ... behold, I am with you till the end of the age" (Matthew 28:18, 20).

Hull (2006) writes that discipleship is God's top priority because Jesus practiced it and commanded His disciples to do it, and His followers continued it.

Bullón (2017) mentions that Jesus began His ministry by making disciples. He did not seek merely believers or church members.

> Jesus began His ministry by making disciples.

Eldon Babcock (2002) indicates that from the very beginning of Jesus's ministry, He was training men to build His kingdom, not to make converts. Making disciples was important to Jesus, and the disciples are essential to the church of today as well.

Our hermeneutic of the Great Commission must be rearticulated. Today, it seems, we have changed the Great Commission. Through our evangelistic campaigns and other activities, we work very hard to make converts, not disciples.

Bullón (2017) adds that no disciple is made in an evangelistic campaign or with the simple exposition of the truth of the Bible. Disciples aren't made in a week or a month. It takes time and life experience. A disciple is a person in constant growth, and growth is not an event but a process.

Evangelistic campaigns are crucial, but they are only the initial part of the process.

Bullón (2017) argues that Paul was aware that the only way new believers would remain true was by sharing their faith.

Hull (2006) quotes Dietrich Bonhoeffer, saying, "Christianity without discipleship is always Christianity without Christ."

I think it's time to pause and reflect on this issue in our lives. It's time to follow the divine plan of life.

A Divine Plan

Making disciples is not a man-made strategy; it's an order from the Lord. This is how the Father proceeds to restore His image in each soul. It's more than just adding new converts to the church. It's God's way of facilitating the

> Making disciples is not a man-made strategy; it's an order from the Lord.

process for every believer to become like Jesus. God wants you to become like Jesus. Isn't that amazing? This is His plan. It must begin in your life right here, right now, to continue into eternity.

John wrote, "Beloved, now we are children of God; and it has not yet been revealed what we shall be, but we know that when He is revealed, we shall be like Him, for we shall see Him as He is" (1 John 3:2 NJKV).

Bullón (2017) argues that the divine plan for evangelism is different from what we are doing now. We cannot forget the divine plan and create our own designs, believing that in this way we are helping God. If we do, we risk reaching the final day and discovering that although we did many good things with the best of intentions, we did not do the Father's will.

Babcock (2002) writes that fulfilling the Great Commission means making disciples, not just making converts. This requires helping people to become disciples.

Paul writes in Ephesians 4:11–12 that the principal role of the church leaders is to prepare the people to do the work of service and ministry so that the body of Christ is built up.

White says, "The only way to grow in grace is to be interestedly doing the very work Christ has enjoined upon us to do."[16] She adds:

Satan summoned all his forces and at every step contested the work of Christ. So, it will be in the great final conflict of the controversy between righteousness and sin. While new life and light and power are descending from high upon the Disciples of Christ, a new life is springing up from beneath and energizing the agencies of Satan.[17]

> Satan summoned all his forces and at every step contested the work of Christ.

> Never does one leave the ranks of evil for the service of God without encountering the assaults of Satan.

You must recognize that you are in a spiritual battle. This fight is real.

White writes, "Never does one leave the ranks of evil for the service of God without encountering the assaults of Satan."[18] That means when a person makes a decision for Jesus and gets baptized, he or she will be prone to satanic attacks.

Usually, after baptism, new converts are left by themselves to go through the motions, to be just members. We leave them by themselves exactly when they need us the most. When they are transitioning to a new life, when they are receiving continual attacks from the enemy, it is precisely at that time that we abandon them. As a result, it is not surprising that so many members leave the church every year. We are wasting many lives. This is where we are losing the battle in the Great Commission.

Moreover, sometimes we underestimate the negative publicity that an ex-member can create against the church. This may have a negative effect on his or her family, friends, and colleagues. It will have a ripple effect. That means when one person leaves the church, it may be more difficult for someone from his or her entourage to come to the church. Discipleship will help a lot in this situation. That is why we must pray to the Lord to help us understand the necessity of discipleship, because when we are disciples of Jesus, we are in love with Jesus. Whatever the challenge we face in life or inside the church, we will never leave Jesus. We will always follow Him.

Personal Application

If you are reading this book, you are indeed chosen by God to understand the necessity for you to be a disciple of Jesus. Because you are a chosen one, God has a marvelous journey before you. Do not settle for little in your spiritual life when God has so much in store for you. Be determined to reach your full potential in Jesus.

Suggested Prayers

1. Jesus, in the darkness and the struggles of my life, open my eyes so I can see the beauty and the peace of walking with You every day as a disciple.
2. The Holy Spirit opens up my mind so I can discover the shallowness of my life and embrace the richness of the life that Jesus offers me today.

CHAPTER 2

---◈--◈--◈---

CHOSEN TO FOLLOW JESUS

"Never does one leave the ranks of evil for the service of God without encountering the assaults of Satan."

—Ellen G. White

Some years ago, in my teenage years, I was extremely sick. I was not able to digest most of the food I ate. I went to many doctors without any results, and my situation was getting worse. One day, my cousin, Dr. Joseph Charles, advised me to see one of his medical professors, one of the top internists at that time. When I went for my appointment, I was surprised that the waiting room was empty. When I asked someone about it, I learned that the doctor had passed out that morning and had been taken to the hospital. I was shocked!

On my way home, I said to myself, "I came to be treated, but the doctor is in worse condition than me." Furthermore, I said to the Lord, "I am not going to take any medicine anymore, O Lord! Either heal me or kill me." (Sorry, but it was my prayer, and I was sincere.) Later, I said to the Lord, "If you heal me, I will become a pastor for you."

One night in my dream, I saw someone like an angel suspended in the air, and he told me, "Give me your arm." I did so, and he used a syringe to draw blood from my arm. When he'd finished, he told me, "You are healed."

From that day on, I had a firm conviction that God had chosen me.

> You also are a chosen person.

You also are a chosen person. What a blessing! You have been chosen by God. The Bible says, "Just as He chose us in Him before the foundation of the world, that we should be holy and without blame before Him in love" (Ephesians 1:4 NKJV).

When Jesus came onto this earth, at the beginning of His ministry, He chose people to follow Him. That was one of Jesus's first moves to save humanity. It also was His last call before leaving this earth. During all His earthly ministry, Jesus kept calling people to be His disciples. That means all the ministry of Jesus was a discipleship ministry.

In the four Gospels, Jesus said "Follow me" around twenty-two times:

- Matthew 4:19; 8:22; 9:9; 10:38; 16:24; 19:21; 19:28
- Mark 1:17; 2:14; 8:34; 10:21
- Luke 5:27; 9:23; 9:59; 18:22
- John 1:43; 8:12; 10:27; 12:26; 13:36; 21:19; 21:22

We can realize that this principle was at the heart of Jesus's call to discipleship. That should be the foundation of the life of any disciple of Jesus.

The call to follow is not only at the beginning of the disciple's life; it must be the lifestyle of the believer until the end.

Case Study: Peter

In Mark 1:17, Jesus asked Peter to follow Him, and Peter left everything to follow Jesus. He spent about three years with Jesus, listening to His teachings, watching His transfiguration, being a witness to His miracles, and spending time with Him in prayer. Peter saw Jesus at least three times after His resurrection, but even so, before Jesus ascended to heaven, He still asked Peter twice—I repeat, *twice*—to follow Him.

> This He spoke, signifying by what death he would glorify God. And when He had spoken this, He said to him, "Follow Me." (John 21:19 NKJV)

> Jesus said to him, "If I will that he remain till I come, what is that to you? You follow Me." (John 21:22 NKJV)

"Following Jesus" is not only for new converts. It's for every believer, every disciple, pastor, or church leader, every day till the end.

"Following Jesus" is not only for new converts. It's for every believer, every disciple, pastor, or church leader, every day till the end. Following Jesus is the journey of your life. This is the only way to stay in God's will. This is the only way to discover your spiritual identity. This is the only way to accomplish the purpose of your life on earth. This is the only way to live in the fullness of your potentiality. It is the process of becoming like Jesus. Every day, listen to this voice: "Follow me." Hull (2006) affirms that we must say every day, "Yes, Jesus, I'll follow you today."

The Meaning of a Disciple

Jesus told us what a disciple is:

> Then He said to them all, "If anyone desires to come after Me, let him deny himself, and take up his cross daily, and follow Me. For whoever desires to save his life will lose it, but whoever loses his life for My sake will save it. For what profit is it to a man if he gains the whole world, and is himself destroyed or lost?" (Luke 9:23–25 NKJV)

For Jesus, a disciple is someone who abides in Him, is obedient, bears fruit, glorifies God, has joy, and loves others. I invite you to meditate on John 15:7–17. Take time to read it and to meditate on it every day. It makes so much sense. The kind of believer who glorifies God best is called a disciple. The last order of Christ to His disciples was to "make disciples" because disciples penetrate the world. Disciples reproduce themselves, which leads to multiplication.

Onyinah (2017) writes that in the scriptures, those who followed Jesus were known as disciples. Afterward, they were named Christians. We find the term "Christian," the Greek *Christonos*, only in three places in the Bible (Acts 11:26, 26:28, 1 Peter 4:16). The New Testament has only nine references to the word "believer," from the Greek word *pistos*.

However, the word "disciples," which comes from the Greek term *mathetes*, is found 261 times in the New Testament. Jesus uses this term Himself in the Gospels.

A tradition of discipleship had been in place long before Jesus came to fulfill His ministry. Hull (2006) gives a brief history of discipleship, saying God chose Joshua, Moses trained him, and then God anointed him (see Deuteronomy 1:38; 31:1–30). Some of Israel's prophets also had followers, or disciples. Isaiah spoke of "my disciples" in Isaiah 8:16. Hull explains:

> The Pharisees also sponsored a formal rabbinical school, and a number of their rabbis became very popular. The reliable Jewish historian Josephus noted that so many young men gathered around rabbis in Herod's day that they were like an army. Gamaliel II reportedly had a thousand disciples who worked on mastering the complicated and extensive Torah. The Pharisees' demanding discipleship system rewarded only the best and brightest and was the doorway to a beautiful religious career.
>
> John the Baptist and his disciples proclaimed a purist form of Judaism that focused on repentance, seeking God, and serving God. John had many disciples, yet only two left him to follow Jesus in the early stages (see John 1:35–50). Many of John's disciples—twelve, in one recorded case (see Acts 19:1–7)— believed in Jesus at a later date. John's semi-monastic disciples were sacrificial; for instance, they were willing to live in the stern realities of the desert.[1]

Hull (2007) affirms that five centuries before Jesus began His ministry, they called a person who was pledged to serve and follow a master teacher a *disciple*. This principle was the same until the time of Jesus. This historical background helps us to understand what Jesus meant when he told his disciples to

> Invariably, discipleship means personal devotion to the master, which molds the life of the *mathetes* (Greek for "disciple."

"make disciples." Jesus will build on and improve His disciples.

Bullón (2017) writes that disciples and believers are not the same. Believers generally read the Bible, attend church, sings hymns, and return tithes, but nothing else. The disciple does all of that *and* follows Jesus, commits to Him, and makes new disciples.

Onyinah (2017) indicates that, generally, a disciple could be considered one who follows the ideas and principles of someone famous and tries to live the way the person lived. In the Christian sense, a disciple is the one growing and yearning to be like Christ and to be conformed to His image.

Hull (2007) notes that, invariably, discipleship means personal devotion to the master, which molds the life of the *mathetes* (Greek for "disciple").

According to Kittel, a disciple is a follower, a student of a confident teacher; John the Baptist, Plato, and Jesus each had disciples. Discipleship always means forming a supremely personal union between the teacher and the follower.

Elliott-Hart declares that Jesus brought the notion of discipleship to an all-new level:

> An additional dimension of the New Testament description of discipleship includes "leaving things behind" to follow Jesus, which goes beyond the typical Hellenistic usage for other philosophical schools. Leaving things behind implies a tremendous commitment which breaks all other ties: for the early companions of the historical Jesus there is both a physical following behind Jesus and the internal commitment to instruction and relationship with Jesus.[2]

> In taking our nature, the Savior has bound Himself to humanity by a tie that is never to be broken.

Through discipleship, God wants us to be closer to Him. White writes, "It was Satan's purpose to bring about an eternal separation between God and man, but in Christ, we become more closely united to God, as if we had never fallen. In taking our nature, the Savior has bound Himself to humanity by a tie that is never to be broken."[3]

The disciple is called to be one with Jesus, united to Him. This is the call of every believer. This is not only a call for new converts; it is the moral duty of every Christian to follow Jesus every day. This is the only way you can be one with Him. He will dwell in you, and you will dwell in Him. This is how you will become like Him.

White adds that when "the disciples came forth from the Savior's training, they were no longer ignorant and uncultured. They had become like Him in mind and character, and other men took knowledge of them, that they had been with Jesus."[4] She writes:

> Under the training of Christ, the disciples had been led to feel their need of the Spirit. Under the Spirit's teaching, they received the final qualification, and went forth to their lifework. No longer were they a collection of independent units or discordant, conflicting elements. No longer were their hopes set on worldly greatness. They were of 'one accord,' 'of one heart and of one soul' (Acts 2:46; 4:32 NKJV). Christ filled their thoughts; the advancement of His kingdom was their aim.[5]

Self-Denial

Self-denial is not easy. Everyone has an ego. But self-denial is the only way we can become disciples of Jesus. Fortunately, God has made a provision for us. The Holy Spirit has power to control the ego so that the beauty of Christ can be seen in our lives. What a joy—what a privilege—that people can see Jesus through our lives.

The good news is that this is God's plan for you. You have been crafted (designed) from eternity to reach this goal.

> Being confident of this very thing, that He who has begun a good work in you will complete it until the day of Jesus Christ (Philippians 1:6 NKJV).

White writes that sin originated in self-seeking.[6] She adds that Jesus gave the condition of discipleship when He said, "If any man will come after Me, let him deny himself, and take up his cross daily, and follow Me."

Abiding in Christ is choosing only the disposition of Christ so that his interests are identified with yours. Abide in him, to be, and to do what he wills. These are the conditions of discipleship, and unless they are complied with, you can never find peace. Peace is in Christ; it cannot be perceived as something apart from Him.[7]

White mentions that Jesus can make a new man or woman of you:

He can mold you into a vessel of honor. You will become a disciple of Christ. You will copy His works, possessing His love and a heart filled with gratitude. You will devote your entire life to Christ, who gave His life for you. You will work, you will suffer, and you will deny self for His sake, even for Him who died and rose again and is making intercessions for you.[8]

White also indicates, "The disciples of Christ had a deep sense of their own inefficiency, and with humiliation and prayer they joined their weakness to His strength, their ignorance to His wisdom, their unworthiness to His righteousness, their poverty to His exhaustless wealth. Thus, strengthened and equipped, they hesitated not to press forward in the service of the Master."[9] She says, "You must be good before you can do good. You cannot exert an influence that will transform others until your own heart has been humbled, refined, and made tender by the grace of Christ."[10]

"True holiness," she adds, "is wholeness in the service of God. This is the condition of true Christian living. Christ asks for an unreserved consecration, for undivided service. He demands the heart, the mind, the soul, and the strength. Self is not to be cherished. He who lives to himself is not a Christian."[11]

Hull (2006) affirms, "When God calls us, He invites us to die." He asks, how do we know God's lives and works in us? The answer comes from Jesus's basic call to discipleship:

> If anyone desires to come after Me, let him deny himself, and take up his cross daily, and follow Me. For whoever desires to save his life will lose it, but whoever loses his life for My sake will save it. For what profit is it to a man if he gains the whole world, and is himself destroyed or lost (Luke 9:23–25 NKJV)?

> If anyone desires to come after Me, let him deny himself, and take up his cross daily, and follow Me.

Committed to a Life of Learning

Nobody can be a disciple of Jesus without committing himself or herself to a life of learning from Him. Paul said, "We know in part" (1 Corinthians 13:9 NKJV). That's why we must be humble enough to continue to learn throughout our lives. After their three years with Jesus, after the resurrection and the Pentecost, the apostles were still in the school of learning to lead the early church. They still maintained their life of prayer. In Acts 6:4, the apostles said, "But we will give ourselves continually to prayer and to the ministry of the word" (NKJV).

White writes, "What privilege, then, was theirs who for three years were in daily contact with that divine life from which has flowed every life-giving impulse that has blessed the world!"[12]

Brown notes, "Another distinctive feature of Jesus's discipleship training is that it was a process, not a program or a project. The disciples continued to grow in faith, even after Jesus was raised from the dead (John 2:22)."[13]

White writes:

> Here is a precious promise. The purposes and plans of God are to be opened to His disciples. What is a disciple? A learner, ever learning. Coming events of a solemn character are opening before us, and God would not have anyone of us think that in these last days, there is no more that we need to know. This is a continual snare of Satan—he would have us meet coming events without special preparation, which is essential to guide us through every difficulty. He would have us stumbling our way along in ignorance, making self-conceit, self-esteem, and self-confidence take the place of true knowledge.[14]

She adds:

> The more satisfied anyone is with himself, and his present knowledge, the less earnestly and humbly will he seek to be guided into all truth. The less of the Holy Spirit of God he has, the more self-satisfied and complacent he will feel. He will not search earnestly and with the most profound interest to know more of truth. But unless he keeps pace with the Leader, who is guiding into all truth, he will be left behind, belated, blinded, confused, because he is not walking in the light … The word

> **The more satisfied anyone is with himself, and his present knowledge, the less earnestly and humbly will he seek to be guided into all truth.**

of God is to be the man of our counsel ... All heaven is looking upon the remnant people of God, to see if they will make truth alone their shield and buckler. Unless the truth is presented as it is in Jesus and is planted in the heart by the power of the Spirit of God, even ministers will be found drifting away from Christ, away from piety, away from religious principle. They will become blind leaders of the blind.[15]

White declares, "Under the guidance of the Holy Spirit, the mind that is devoted unreservedly to God develops harmoniously and is strengthened to comprehend and fulfill the requirements of God. The weak, vacillating character becomes changed to one of strength and steadfastness. Continual devotion establishes so close a relation between Jesus and His disciple that the Christian becomes like Him in mind and character."[16]

Depending on God

From His baptism to the cross, Jesus always depended on God to do everything. In the same way, throughout all of his or her life, the disciple must depend on God for every turn and twist of the mission. At the moment when we start following our own wills, we cease to be disciples of Jesus.

White writes:

There have ever been in the church those who are always inclined toward individual independence. They seem unable to realize that independence of spirit is liable to lead the human agent to have too much confidence in himself and to trust in his own judgment rather than to respect the counsel and highly esteem the judgment of his brethren, especially of those in the offices that God has appointed for the leadership of His people. God has invested His church with special authority and power which no one can be justified in disregarding and despising, for he who does this despises the voice of God.[17]

She adds, "Like the disciples, we are in danger of losing sight of our dependence on God … We need to look constantly to Jesus, realizing that it is His power that does the work. While we are to labor earnestly for the salvation of the lost, we also must take time for meditation, for prayer, and for the study of the Word of God. Only the work accomplished with much prayer, and sanctified by the merit of Christ, will in the end prove to have been efficient for good."[18]

His Usage of the Word

The disciple should develop a special love for the scriptures—that is where we will know Jesus better. Jesus said, "You search the Scriptures, for in them you think you have eternal life; and these are they which testify of Me" (John 5:39 NKJV). There is the Word of God for our lives. Paul wrote, "All Scripture is given by inspiration of God, and is profitable for doctrine, for reproof, for correction, for instruction in righteousness" (2 Timothy 3:16 NKJV). In the temptation story found in Matthew 4:1–11, we can see that Jesus gained victory over the devil by using the scriptures. There will be no chance to live a victorious life without the scriptures. Jesus's disciples must develop a special love for the Bible and read it every day.

When we consider the vital role of the Bible in the life of Jesus, we can understand how the disciple should recognize the importance of the Bible for his or her everyday life.

Jesus uses the Bible as the center of His ministry. He began His ministry by reading the Bible (Luke 4:16–21). He used it in the temptation (Matthew 4:4); in discussion with the Jews (John 12:47–49); to teach the people (John 5:39, 10:35); on the cross (Matthew 27:46, Psalm 22:2); and after His resurrection, with the two disciples on the road to and from Emmaus (Luke 24:13–35).

Jesus says, "If you abide in My word, you are My disciples indeed. And you shall know the truth, and the truth shall make you free" (John 8:31–32 NKJV).

White writes that we can overcome the wicked one by the way in which Christ overcame—the power of the Word.[19] She adds that the followers of Jesus are not in the will of God if they are content to remain in ignorance of His Word. All should become Bible students.

Christ commands His followers, "Search the scriptures; for in them ye think ye have eternal life: and they are they which testify of me" (John 5:39 NKJV).

Peter exhorts us, "But sanctify the Lord God in your hearts, and be ready always to give an answer to every man that asketh you a reason of the hope that is in you with meekness and fear" (1 Peter 3:15 NKJV).

Bullón (2017) declares that through daily Bible study, we develop a fellowship with Jesus. The result is the transformation of the disciple into the likeness of Christ. Paul says, "But we all, with unveiled face, beholding as in a mirror the glory of the Lord, are being transformed into the same image from glory to glory, just as by the Spirit of the Lord" (2 Corinthians 3:18 NKJV). To contemplate the "Lord's glory" is not a mystical experience. It's not an act of transcendental meditation. It is a practical experience of fellowshipping.

His Empowerment of the Holy Spirit

There could not be any disciples without the work of the Holy Spirit in our lives. From the first to the last book of the Bible, you can see the importance of the Holy Spirit.

The Holy Spirit is not a force or an influence; He is a person. "He may be grieved (Ephesians 4:30), He may be quenched in terms of the exercise of His will (1 Thessalonians 5:19), and He may be resisted (Acts 7:51)."[20] He is God.

Paul wrote:

> But God has revealed them to us through His Spirit. For the Spirit searches all things, yes, the deep things of God. For what man knows the things of a man except the spirit of the man which is in him? Even so no one knows the things of God except the Spirit of God (1 Corinthians 2:10–11 NKJV).

He will teach you because He is "the Helper, the Holy Spirit, whom the Father will send in My name, He will teach you all things" (John 14:26 NKJV). Only He can guide us in all the truth. "However, when He, the Spirit of truth, has come, He will guide you into all truth" (John 16:13 NKJV).

From the beginning of His ministry until the end, Jesus was filled with the Holy Spirit.

So, He came to Nazareth, where He had been brought up. And as His custom was, He went into the synagogue on the Sabbath day and stood up to read. And He was handed the book of the prophet Isaiah. And when He had opened the book, He found the place where it was written:

"The Spirit of the Lord is upon Me,

Because He has anointed Me to preach the gospel to the poor;

He has sent Me to heal the brokenhearted,

To proclaim liberty to the captives

And recovery of sight to the blind,

To set at liberty those who are oppressed;

To proclaim the acceptable year of the Lord."

Then He closed the book, and gave it back to the attendant and sat down. And the eyes of all who were in the synagogue were fixed on Him. And He began to say to them, "Today this Scripture is fulfilled in your hearing." (Luke 4:16–21 NKJV)

Even on the cross, the Holy Spirit was with Jesus to help Him in His sufferings:

For if the blood of bulls and goats and the ashes of a heifer, sprinkling the unclean, sanctifies for the purifying of the flesh, how much more shall the blood of Christ, who through the eternal Spirit offered Himself without spot to God, cleanse your conscience from dead works to serve the living God (Hebrews 9:13–14 NJKV)?

White writes, "God takes men as they are and educates them for His service if they will yield themselves to Him. The Spirit of God, received into the soul, will quicken all its faculties. Under the guidance of the Holy Spirit, the mind that is devoted unreservedly to God develops harmoniously, and is strengthened to comprehend and fulfill the requirements of God."[21]

> Wherever the Holy Spirit dwells, His holy presence creates a hunger for holiness.

Donald Whitney (2014) writes, "Wherever the Holy Spirit dwells, His holy presence creates a hunger for holiness. His primary task is to magnify Christ (see John 16:14–15), and He begins to carry out the will of God to make the child of God like the Son of God (see Romans 8:29)."[22]

Self-control, according to Galatians 5:23, is a direct product of the Spirit's control in the believer's life. When the Christian expresses this Spirit-produced self-control by practicing the spiritual disciplines, the result is progress in godliness. White affirms, "The Holy Spirit is the breath of spiritual life in the soul."[23]

Onyinah (2017) says, "The principal resources God has given to His people to disciple others include the Holy Spirit, who is always with them (Luke 24:49; Acts 1:8); His Word, which is still available to them (John 15:1–17); and spiritual gifts that are available to them (Ephesians 4:11–16; 1 Corinthians 12:7–11). The Holy Spirit is the life force of the disciple's evangelistic zeal. Without the Holy Spirit, there is no witness (Acts 1:8)."[24]

The disciple of Jesus must seek to be filled with the Holy Spirit every day. Without the Holy Spirit, nobody can follow Jesus.

His Life of Prayer

The life of Jesus was a life of prayer. From the beginning of His ministry through the end, we can see Jesus in prayer. We cannot be a disciple of Jesus without a life of prayer.

White declares, "At the eventide or in the early morning, Jesus went away to the sanctuary of the mountains for communion with His Father. Often, He passed the entire night in prayer and meditation, returning at daybreak to His work among the people."[25] She adds, "The Redeemer had spent entire nights praying for His disciples, that their faith might not fail."[26]

She says:

> The disciples prayed that greater strength might be imparted to them in the work of the ministry, for they saw that they would meet the same determined opposition that Christ had encountered when upon the earth. While their united prayers were ascending in faith to heaven, the answer came. The place where they were assembled was shaken, and they were endowed anew with the Holy Spirit. Their hearts filled with courage; they again went forth to proclaim the word of God in Jerusalem. "With great power gave the apostles witness of the resurrection of the Lord Jesus," and God marvelously blessed their efforts.[27]

White writes, "When this reformation begins, the spirit of prayer will actuate every believer and will banish from the church the spirit of discord and strife."[28]

Jesus told us, "Ask what you desire, and it shall be done for you" (John 15:7 NKJV).

Hull (2007) writes that the disciple learns to talk to God by listening to what God says first. Prayer responds to what God has already said. Remaining in Christ requires both God's Word and prayer.

Bullón (2017) affirms that we must have intercessors in our churches. Jesus knew that the disciples, however well-intentioned, were doomed to defeat if they attempted to walk the Christian journey by themselves. So, He prayed for us.

> We must have intercessors in our churches.

> "Simon, Simon! Indeed, Satan has asked for you, that he may sift you as wheat. But I have prayed for you, that your faith should not fail; and when you have returned to Me, strengthen your brethren" (Luke 22:31–32 NKJV).

There are two components to this text. First, Jesus felt compassion for Peter and His other disciples and prayed for them. To Peter, He said, "I have prayed for you, Simon, that your faith may not fail." Then He gives him an order: "And when you have turned back, strengthen your brothers."

Jesus's prayer life teaches us not only to pray without ceasing but also to pray for others. The disciple is an intercessor.

His Obedience

Jesus was obedient to His Father.

> He went a little farther and fell on His face, and prayed, saying, "O My Father, if it is possible, let this cup pass from Me; nevertheless, not as I will, but as You will" (Matthew 26:39 NKJV).

White writes that "to be a Christian is to become a disciple of Christ. That means obedience, and nothing short of this will be accepted."[29]

She affirms that "obedience is the test of discipleship. But how little do men appreciate the privilege of having the companionship of Christ, of being in harmony with God! They do not realize that they are Christ's property, bought with an infinite price and that they are to glorify God in their body and in their spirits, which are his. The most important friendship is the friendship of God."[30]

William Whitmore (2018) mentions that Bonhoeffer's understanding of discipleship requires the individual believer—and the church as a whole—to choose to follow Christ. Once this decision has been finalized, the disciple is to be obedient to God.

His Humility

In this world of materialism, it is hard to practice humility. White mentions, "I am thankful that God is a wise ruler, and everyone who is a true disciple of Christ will be humble, lift his cross, and meekly follow where the self-denying, self-sacrificing Jesus leads the way."[31]

In Philippians 2.1–11, Paul writes about the humility of Jesus:

Then Jesus said to them, "When you lift up the Son of Man, then you will know that I am He, and that I do nothing of Myself; but as My Father taught Me, I speak these things. And He who sent Me is with Me. The Father has not left Me alone, for I always do those things that please Him." As He spoke these words, many believed in Him (John 8:28–30 NKJV).

Jesus said, "I do not seek My own glory" (John 8:50 NKJV).

He who speaks from himself seeks his own glory; but He who seeks the glory of the One who sent Him is true, and no unrighteousness is in Him (John 7:18 NKJV).

Paul writes, "Yet indeed I also count all things loss for the excellence of the knowledge of Christ Jesus my Lord, for whom I have suffered the loss of all things, and count them as rubbish, that I may gain Christ" (Philippians 3:8 NKJV).

The disciple will always look to the humility of His Master. The disciple must be humble.

His Love

The story of Jesus is a lover's story. He accepted coming to this earth to suffer and to die only because He loves us. In return, He asks His disciples to love.

These things I command you, that you love one another (John 15:17 NKJV).

Love is the ultimate test to prove you are Jesus's disciple. Jesus said, "By this all will know that you are My disciples, if you have love for one another" (John 13:35 NKJV). We will have a love for others through the

Holy Spirit. We read in Galatians 5:22–23, "But the fruit of the Spirit is love, joy, peace, longsuffering, kindness, goodness, faithfulness, gentleness, self-control. Against such there is no law" (NKJV).

As Jesus's disciples, we must show love to others because God is love. Never forget—love is greater than faith and prophecy.

To be Christ's disciple, you must follow Him every day in every aspect of your life. This is your calling. You are called to follow Him in your family, your job, at church, and wherever you are. This is how you will discover your true identity. This is how you will understand why you were born on this earth. And the more you follow Jesus, the more you will become like Him.

Personal Application

In these last days, I want to be one of the disciples of Jesus, asking Him to help me deny myself and learn from Him daily. I want Jesus to reshape my spiritual life. From today on, I want to live for Jesus, not for myself.

Suggested Prayers

1. Holy Spirit, help me to deny myself every day and to let Jesus live in me.
2. O Jesus, I give You my life again today. Take my weak hand in Your mighty

Hands. I want to follow You every day.

3. Dear Jesus! Baptize me every day with the Holy Spirit so I can be an obedient disciple.

CHAPTER 3

---◆—◆—◆---

CHOSEN TO BE LIKE JESUS

"At the eventide or in the early morning, Jesus went away to the sanctuary of the mountains for communion with His Father. Often, He passed the entire night in prayer and meditation, returning at daybreak to His work among the people."
—Ellen G. White

One day, my wife was scheduled to work on a Saturday night. Before she went to the hospital, she felt that she had to pray, and she also asked some friends to pray for her. Upon her arrival on the floor, it was calm, and some patients were talking to each other. After she entered the nurses' station and was waiting to get a daily report, she was called for help. A patient, who had been calm earlier, had started acting out. She went to the room, where the other patients said, "It's because of you."

The patients were pulling their hair and yelling. After they calmed down, my wife found that the patients had been having a meeting on how to become Satanists. The presence of Christ, through His servant, my wife, had disturbed the ceremony.

When you are a disciple of Jesus, He gives you power over all demons.

Then the seventy returned with joy, saying, "Lord, even the demons are subject to us in Your name." And He said to them, "I saw Satan fall like lightning from heaven. Behold, I give you the authority to trample on serpents and scorpions, and over all the power of the enemy, and nothing shall by any means hurt you. Nevertheless, do not rejoice in this, that the spirits are subject to you, but rather rejoice because your names are written in heaven" (Luke 10:17–20 NKJV).

We are God's ambassadors on this earth.

I would like you to understand that God wants us to be like Jesus. This is the ultimate goal of all redemptive plans. That's why Jesus came and died on this earth. This goal reaches every believer. God only wants your will, your availability, and your disposition, and He will do the rest through the Holy Spirit. Jesus said, "Abide in Me, and I in you" (John 15:4 NKJV).

Chosen to Bear Fruit

It is not fitting just to say that we are Christians. People must see that in our lives. In other words, the disciple of Jesus is supposed to bear fruit. The disciple bears fruit for God's glory.

Onyinah (2017) affirms that one of the marks of disciples is that they bear fruit for Christ. That is well demonstrated in John 15:1–17, where Jesus's disciples are said to "bear fruit," "more fruit," and "much fruit," and that "fruit should remain" (John 15:2, 5, 8, 16 NKJV). Jesus states, "By this, My Father is glorified, that you bear much fruit; so you will be My disciples" (John 15:8 NKJV).

Onyinah (2017) adds:

There are two kinds of fruit. First is the fruit of character. Disciples need to be like their Master in character. The character of Christ is depicted by the fruit of the Spirit— "love, joy, peace, longsuffering, kindness, goodness, faithfulness, gentleness, self-control" (Galatians 5:22–23 NKJV). In today's Christianity, people tend to desire the power to perform supernatural acts. Many people are attracted to those who claim to be miracle workers, hailing such people as more spiritual. Although the promise of power exists in Jesus's sayings (John 14:12; Acts 1:8), the evidence of true spirituality is demonstrated in the transformation of character, which includes one's entire attitude, outlook, and relationship with others (Matthew 7:22–23; John 13:35).[1]

Onyinah continues, "Secondly, there is the fruit by way of influencing the lives of others for Christ. Every fruit contains a seed that guarantees its reproduction. The disciples are expected to reproduce their kind. They must win others to Christ and disciple them to maturity so that those won will also bear fruit and make the cycle continue."[2]

Babcock (2002) writes that Paul lived out the admonition of 2 Timothy 2:2:

Paul reproduced himself in the battle with soldiers like Timothy, Titus, Silus (Silvanus), Euodia, Syntyche, Epaphroditus, Priscilla, and Aquila. Paul called Timothy his true son in the faith and instructed Timothy to follow his instructions so that in obeying them, he would be able to fight the good fight of faith (1 Timothy 2:18).

By this, My Father is glorified, that you bear much fruit (John 15:8 NKJV).

> There is work for you to do in the church and out of the church.

White writes that there is work for you to do in the church and out of the church: "The fruit we bear is the only test of the character of the tree before the world. This is proof of our discipleship. If our works are of such a character that, as branches of the Living Vine, we bear rich clusters of precious fruit, then we bear before the world God's own badge as His sons and daughters. We are living epistles, known and read of all men."[3]

The other distinctive element of Jesus's call to discipleship is holiness. Jesus said, "Sanctify them by Your truth. Your word is truth" (John 17:17 NKJV). He added, "And for their sakes, I sanctify Myself, that they also may be sanctified by the truth" (John 17:19 NKJV).

Brown (2012) says, "This distinguishing mark not only identifies the new character of the believer, but it also identifies the eternal purpose of God." Paul wrote, "He chose us in Him before the foundation of the world, that we should be holy and without blame before Him in love" (Ephesians 1:4 NKJV). It is essential to recognize that holiness is the aim of God's call for all Christians, not just a few "super-Christians."

> But as He who called you is holy, you also be holy in all your conduct, because it is written, "Be holy, for I am holy" (1 Peter 1:15–16 NKJV).

Chosen to Love

Cole (2018) writes that the Great Commandment is the call to love, fueling the work of the Great Commission with that love. The process of love was started by God in His missionary plan to love humankind back into a relationship with Him.

Bullón (2017) affirms that God's church is the church of love. Love is its main feature. Because of its love for God, it follows His instructions and advice, and because of its love for human beings, it enters into a loveless world to bring people to Jesus.

White writes that love is the evidence of discipleship.[4]

> By this all will know that you are My disciples, if you have love for one another (John 13:35 NKJV).

Hull (2007) argues that disciples love as Christ loves. Jesus said, "This is My commandment, that you love one another as I have loved you. Greater love has no one than this, than to lay down one's life for his friends … These things I command you, that you love one another" (John 15:12–13, 17 NKJV).

> Paul gives us the hymn of biblical love:

> Love suffers long and is kind; love does not envy; love does not parade itself, is not puffed up; does not behave rudely, does not seek its own, is not provoked, thinks no evil; does not rejoice in iniquity, but rejoices in the truth; bears all things, believes all things, hopes all things, endures all things.

> Love never fails. But whether there are prophecies, they will fail; whether there are tongues, they will cease; whether there is knowledge, it will vanish away. For we know in part and we prophesy in part. But when that which is perfect has come, then that which is in part will be done away.

When I was a child, I spoke as a child, I understood as a child, I thought as a child; but when I became a man, I put away childish things. For now, we see in a mirror, dimly, but then face to face. Now I know in part, but then I shall know just as I also am known.

And now abide faith, hope, love, these three; but the greatest of these is love (1 Corinthians 13:4–13).

Chosen to Live in the Likeness of Jesus

The ultimate goal of each disciple is to become like Jesus. This idea is derived from several passages in the New Testament. In his letter to the Galatians, Paul wrote, "Until Christ is formed in you" (Galatians 4:19 NKJV). The English word "form" is from the Greek *morph*, which means to shape. In 2 Corinthians 3:18, Paul wrote, "But we all, with unveiled face, beholding as in a mirror the glory of the Lord, are being transformed (*metamorphóomai*) into the same image from glory to glory, just as by the Spirit of the Lord" (NKJV). This verse makes it evident that spiritual evolution is a divine work carried out by the Holy Spirit. We do not have a physical fellowship with Jesus like the one enjoyed by the first twelve disciples; ours is a spiritual one.

> The ultimate goal of each disciple is to become like Jesus.

Bullón (2017) affirms that when Jesus called His disciples, He wanted them to be like Him. True disciples are like their Master and do what their Master does. Paul became a disciple of Christ and then wrote to the Corinthians, "Imitate me, just as I also imitate Christ" (1 Corinthians 11:1 NKJV). And to the Philippians, he wrote, "Brethren, join in following my example, and note those who so walk, as you have us for a pattern" (Philippians 3:17 NKJV). Paul dared to make such a statement because he had a conviction. "I have been crucified with Christ; it is no longer I who live, but Christ lives in me; and the life which I now live in the flesh I live by faith in the Son of God, who loved me and gave Himself for me" (Galatians 2:20 NKJV). And how did Paul reach such an experience? Through daily fellowship with Jesus.

Onyinah (2017) writes that the ultimate aim of disciples, as has been stated, is to be like the Master. To become like one's Master, that individual must hold onto the Master's teachings.

Hull (2007) declares that Jesus willingly took on our humanity; we need to take on Christlikeness voluntarily.

Onyinah (2017) affirms that although Christlikeness is the ultimate goal of the disciple (1 Corinthians 11:1; Ephesians 4:13, 15, 20; Colossians 1:28), God uses human agents in this transformational work (1 Corinthians 4:16–17; 11:1). The human agent already must have become a disciple, as whether for good or bad, the disciple will become like his teacher (Luke 6:40). Thus, it is essential for every believer discipling another to exhibit the traits that Jesus possessed.

Brown (2012) declares that finally, the goal of discipleship is to transform the believer into the likeness of Jesus. "For whom He foreknew, He also predestined to be conformed to the image of His Son, that He might be the firstborn among many brethren" (Romans 8:29 NKJV).

Hull (2007) mentions that in John 15:7–17, Jesus teaches that His relationship to the disciples is like that of a vine to the branches.

Sin tries to darken the image of God in human souls. Discipleship is the divine way to restore God's image in us. We can understand why the enemy will do all in his power to push God's people to neglect or overlook discipleship.

White declares, "Those who profess to be disciples of Christ should be elevated in all their thoughts and acts, and should ever realize that they are fit for immortality; and that, if saved, they must be without spot, or wrinkle, or any such thing. Their Christian characters must be without a blemish, or they will be pronounced unfit to be taken to heaven, to dwell with pure, sinless beings in God's everlasting kingdom."[5]

She adds that God "gives the Holy Spirit to help in every strait, to strengthen our hope and assurance, to illuminate our minds and purify our hearts."[6]

> Discipleship is not another method or program. It is God's command in the great controversy to restore His image in His children.

To sum up, we can say that Jesus wants us to be like Him. At the end of His ministry, before ascending to heaven, Jesus gave the Great Commission with a particular emphasis, asking His followers to make disciples. Discipleship is not another method or program. It is God's command in the great controversy to restore His image in His children. But to persevere in this remarkable journey, you need some spiritual disciplines.

Personal Application

The Holy Spirit has the influence and authority to make anybody become like Jesus. If you do not become like Jesus, it's not God's fault. It's your responsibility. What goal can be more enjoyable than that one? After all, this is your destiny, and very soon, you will be with Jesus forever.

Suggested Prayers

1. O God, I understand that You want me to be like Jesus. Accomplish this goal in my life by Your grace.
2. O Jesus, help me to be like You in my family, my job, my church, and all aspects of my everyday life.

PART II

HOW TO BE A DISCIPLE?

CHAPTER 4

---◆--◆--◆---

CHOSEN TO PRACTICE SPIRITUAL DISCIPLINES

"Meditation and prayer would keep us from rushing unbidden into the way of danger,
and thus we should be saved from many a defeat."

—Ellen G. White

Those who have spent time in worship, prayer, or fasting can testify to the joy that they experience after those moments. One day, on my way back home after a day of worship, I was with my wife, Gina, and daughter, Daniela. After a quick comment on the day, Daniela fell asleep. I was talking to Gina regarding the worship of the day. We both were immensely blessed by the main text of the sermon, found in Luke 9:1— "Then He called His twelve disciples together and gave them power and authority over all demons, and to cure diseases" (NKJV). It was like a new revelation to us. We understood better what capabilities Jesus gives to His disciples. This verse helped me all week. Worship is one of the spiritual disciplines for the disciple. Spiritual disciplines will help you to find God in this noisy world and give you clarity of mind. Spiritual disciplines are the way to keep your fellowship with Jesus.

Last year, a group of five pastors, including myself, went to Mexico. We were delighted to see each other again. The itinerary was from JFK Airport, New York, to Monterrey, Mexico, with a short layover in Mexico City. During that time, we laughed together, talking about almost everything. Pastors love talking. The time came to leave Mexico City for Monterrey. We were in line for the final check before boarding the plane. Airline staff at the checkpoint looked at our boarding passes but stopped one of us, saying to that pastor that his flight had already left. Four of us had Flight 910, but for this particular pastor, his flight number was 906. He had missed his flight.

That was a shock and a surprise for the group, but it could happen easily to me or to any one of us. We were together, enjoying the time. We were relying on one another without taking the time to look attentively at our personal boarding passes.

In this life, you are unique; each of us has a specific itinerary. To not miss your flight, you must take out a special time each day to look at your personal itinerary with Jesus.

Even though you might feel fine and think everything is okay, if you do not take time to listen to Jesus every day, you could miss the dream that the Lord has designed specifically for your life. That is where spiritual disciplines may help.

Spiritual disciplines will help you find God in a noisy world. Spiritual disciplines are the way to keep your fellowship with Jesus.

Harrington (2017) quotes Kevin DeYoung, writing that nobody achieves the highest level in sports without working out. Nobody can make it in music without lots of practice. Nobody will shine in knowledge without lengthy study. And in the school of holiness, nobody can go far without hours and days and years in studying the Bible.

Hull (2006) writes that the road to godliness is a road of discipline. He adds that the spiritual disciplines are a necessary part of believing and following Christ.

> The road to godliness is a road of discipline.

Lynn (2014) affirms that spiritual disciplines are behaviors or habits that someone practices to be more like Christ. The apostle Paul asked his young follower Timothy to be disciplined to reach godliness. Paul writes, "Reject profane and old wives' fables, and exercise yourself toward godliness" (1 Timothy 4:7 NKJV).

The word Paul uses is the word "discipline" or *train* in Greek (Γύμναζε) that can be translated as *gymnaze*, from which we get our English word "gymnasium." The Holy Spirit knows that we need exercise and discipline in our life as disciples.

Discipline implies time and effort. Lynn writes, "Spiritual disciplines such as prayer, reading the Word of God, community (or fellowship), fasting, and worship practiced over a significant period brings forth a changed life."[1]

Being a disciple of Jesus requires spiritual discipline.

Paul said, "Everyone who competes for the prize is temperate in all things. Now they do it to obtain a perishable crown, but we for an imperishable crown" (1 Corinthians 9:25 NKJV). Here we can see the Holy Spirit encourages believers to practice certain disciplines in their spiritual lives.

Second Timothy 2:5 is another text on spiritual disciplines, where Paul says anyone who competes as an athlete does not receive the victor's crown except by competing according to the rules.

Brown (2012) writes, "Spiritual disciplines are those intentional and regular biblical practices of Christ-followers that position them before God so that He can transform them"; in short, they are tools for training that "develop intimacy for God and fitness for serving. ... The spiritual disciplines include, but are not limited to, Bible reading, prayer, fasting, serving, giving, journaling, and worship."[2]

Travis (1965) argues that discipline is the ongoing work of discipleship. We can see in Jesus's life the model and motivation for a disciplined life.

White writes, "God expects His church to discipline and fit its members for the work of enlightening the world."[3]

Whitney (2014) mentions that discipline is at the heart of discipleship. This is validated by 2 Timothy 1:7, which says, "God has not given us a spirit of fear, but of power and of love and of a sound mind." A vital component of this self-control in a follower of Jesus is spiritual self-discipline, as Paul said in Galatians 5:22–23.

Whitney (2014) affirms that not many great things could be accomplished without discipline. Many professionals and other people have been ruined because they abandoned discipline and let themselves grow slack.

Hull (2006) argues that the spiritual disciplines are a necessary part of believing and following Christ. Whitney (2014) suggests disciplining yourself to find the time to devote to the spiritual disciplines. Try to make it the same time every day.

White writes, "If men endure the necessary discipline, without complaining or fainting by the way, God will teach them hour by hour, and day by day."[4]

Chisholm (2016) affirms that disciples cannot grow and mature in faith unless they intentionally engage in spiritual practices and commit themselves firmly to a congregation of fellow disciples. Disciple-making cannot happen by accident because it is a spiritual discipline.

Jesus explains the process of making disciples. We need to earnestly seek out occasions to share the gospel (Mark 16:15), baptize people, and train them on how to obey everything that Jesus commanded (Matthew 28:19–20).

Whitney (2014) writes that "for [the disciples] to follow Jesus required discipline. They had to go where He went and when. Following Jesus today and learning from Him still involves discipline, for you don't follow someone accidentally—at least not for very long—nor do you learn as much accidentally as you do by discipline. Are you a disciplined follower of Jesus?"[5]

> Spiritual discipline must be a way of life because the devil will use every weapon possible to fight us.

Spiritual discipline must be a way of life because the devil will use every weapon possible to fight us. White writes, "Often when Satan has failed of exciting distrust, he succeeds in leading us to presumption."[6]

Whitney (2014) affirms that the essential feature of any spiritual discipline is its objective, so there is low value in practicing spiritual disciplines apart from the single goal of godliness.

Lynn (2014) mentions that the main reason there is a considerable gap between what Christians believe and how they behave is the lack of spiritual discipline in the lives of the followers of Christ.

White writes, "Satan makes every effort to lead people away from God; and he is successful in his purpose when the religious life is drowned in business cares, when he can so absorb their minds in business that they will not take time to read their Bibles, to pray in secret, and to keep the offering of praise and thanksgiving burning on the altar of sacrifice, morning and evening."[7]

In this chapter, we will consider the following spiritual disciplines: daily Bible reading and meditation, prayer, fasting, worship, stewardship, and evangelism.

Daily Bible Reading and Meditation

Reading the Bible and meditating is a necessary daily activity for those who want to follow Jesus.

> Among people who claim to be "born-again Christians," only 18% read the Bible daily.

Whitney (2014) notes a survey taken by the Barna Research Group, which disclosed these disheartening numbers: among people who claim to be "born-again Christians," only 18% read the Bible daily. "Worst of all, 23 percent—almost one in four professing Christians—say they never read the Word of God."[8]

In 2 Timothy 3:16, Paul writes, "All Scripture is given by inspiration of God, and is profitable for doctrine, for reproof, for correction, for instruction in righteousness" (NKJV). Whitney (2014) writes that no spiritual discipline is more important than the intake of God's Word. Nothing can be substituted for it.

Hull (2010) affirms that the Bible will help us to know the ways and the will of God. The bare bones of every spiritual discipline are rooted in scripture. Only God's Word can help us grow spiritually.

Brandon Hilgemann (2018) writes, "Jesus understood the Bible better than anyone. As a boy, he astonished the rabbis in the Jerusalem temple with his knowledge (Luke 2:46–47). He cited scripture when He was tempted in the wilderness (Luke 4:1–13). And he continually quoted it in his instructions (see Matthew 5:21; Mark 10:5–9). He began his ministry with a public reading from the book of Isaiah (Luke 4:16–21). Jesus personifies the Word (John 1:14)."[9]

Today, more than ever, we must practice the discipline of studying and meditating on the Word of God. Psalm 119:97 says, "Oh, how I love Your law! It is my meditation all the day" (NKJV).

White writes that all Jesus's strength is yours.[10]

> Your word I have hidden in my heart, that I might not sin against You. (Psalm 119:11 NKJV)

> By the word of Your lips, I have kept away from the paths of the destroyer. (Psalm 17:4 NKJV)

White tells us, "By the word of God succor was given to the Hebrew host, and by the same word it would be given to Jesus. He awaited God's time to bring relief. He was in the wilderness in obedience to God, and He would not obtain food by following the suggestions of Satan. In the presence of the witnessing universe, He testified that it is of less calamity to suffer whatever may befall than to depart in any manner from the will of God."[11]

> And you shall remember that the Lord your God led you all the way these forty years in the wilderness, to humble you and test you, to know what was in your heart, whether you would keep His commandments or not. So He humbled you, allowed you to hunger, and fed you with manna which you did not know nor did your fathers know, that He might make you know that man shall not live by bread alone; but man lives by every word that proceeds from the mouth of the Lord. (Deuteronomy 8:2–3 NKJV)

White writes, "In every temptation, the weapon of God's warfare was the word of God."[12] She adds:

The followers of Jesus are not meeting the mind and will of God if they are content to remain in ignorance of His Word. All should become Bible students. Christ commanded His followers, "Search the Scriptures; for in them ye think ye have eternal life: and they are

> The followers of Jesus are not meeting the mind and will of God if they are content to remain in ignorance of His Word.

they which testify of Me." Peter exhorts us, "But sanctify the Lord God in your hearts, and be ready always to answer every man that asketh you a reason of the hope that is in you with meekness and fear."[13]

White affirms, "It was by the word of God that Christ overcame the wicked one."[14]

Bullón (2017) writes that a disciple needs to know and trust the Word of God to make other disciples. It is not simply theoretical knowledge. If I have a doctoral degree and spend most of my time studying the divine mysteries and writing about them but do not live out biblical truths or influence others to become disciples, I am not a disciple. I may be a scholar, but I'm not a disciple. A disciple is one who knows the Bible and applies it to daily living and to making disciples out of other persons.

White writes that meditation and prayer will "keep us from rushing unbidden into the way of danger, and thus we should be saved from many a defeat."[15]

We must read and meditate on the Bible every day. Many verses of the Bible show the importance of daily reading of and meditation on the scriptures.

God gives the promise of success to those who read daily the scriptures and put them into practice. He said, "This Book of the Law shall not depart from your mouth, but you shall meditate in it day and night, that you may observe to do according to all that is written in it. For then you will make your way prosperous, and then you will have good success" (Joshua 1:8 NKJV).

In Psalm 1:1–3, we read:

> Blessed is the man
>
> Who walks not in the counsel of the ungodly,
>
> Nor stands in the path of sinners,
>
> Nor sits in the seat of the scornful;
>
> But his delight is in the law of the Lord,
>
> And in His law, he meditates day and night.
>
> He shall be like a tree
>
> Planted by the rivers of water,
>
> That brings forth its fruit in its season,
>
> Whose leaf also shall not wither;
>
> And whatever he does shall prosper. (NKJV)

Psalm 119:97–101 tells us:

> Oh, how I love Your law!
>
> It is my meditation all the day.
>
> You, through Your commandments, make me wiser than my enemies;
>
> For they are ever with me.
>
> I have more understanding than all my teachers,
>
> For Your testimonies are my meditation.
>
> I understand more than the ancients,
>
> Because I keep Your precepts.
>
> I have restrained my feet from every evil way,
>
> That I may keep Your word. (NKJV)

It is also important to memorize some verses of the Bible. Whitney (2014) explains, "There is no better illustration of this than Jesus's confrontation with Satan in the lonely Judean wilderness (see Matthew 4:1–11). Each time the enemy thrust a temptation at Jesus, He parried it with the Sword of the Spirit. It was the Spirit-prompted recollection of specific texts of scripture that helped Jesus experience victory. One of the ways we can experience more spiritual victories is to do as Jesus did—memorize scripture so that it is within us for the Holy Spirit to bring to our remembrance when it's needed."

A Weapon against Fanaticism

White writes, "In 1844, we had to meet fanaticism on every hand, but always the word came to me: A great wave of excitement is an injury to the work. Keep your feet in the footprints of Christ."[16]

She adds:

> [As] the end draws near, the enemy will work with all his power to bring in fanaticism among us. He would rejoice to see Seventh-day Adventists going to such extremes that they would be branded by the world as a body of fanatics. Against this danger, I am bidden to warn ministers and lay members. Our work is to teach men and women to build on a true foundation, to plant their feet on a plain "Thus saith the Lord."[17]

White affirms, "Satan is a diligent Bible student. He knows that his time is short, and he seeks at every point to counter the work of the Lord upon this earth."[18]

Prayer

Some time ago, my wife's niece was pregnant, and one Saturday in the month of her due date, she went to the doctor for a routine check. The doctor told her that the baby was not breathing. Later, they found out that the baby had died inside her. The doctor accused her of not paying attention to the movement of the baby. She was sent to the hospital immediately for a follow-up. She stayed at the hospital for two days and did not have any strong contractions despite being given an IV with Pitocin. On Sunday, the doctor decided to discontinue the Pitocin IV and to restart it on Monday.

The family was told that the mother was at risk for infection because the baby had been dead in her womb for about three days. The family was in prayer, asking God to save the mother and to deliver the baby without a C-section.

While some members of the family were praying, on Sunday night at around eleven o'clock, one of them had a vision and saw Jesus landing. He put His left foot first at the side of the mother's bed. Jesus was wearing hospital scrubs, and He intervened. At around 11:45, the mother said that she felt hot and started having contractions. She had the strength to push, and she expelled the dead baby with no human help.

> Yes! There is power in prayer.

> The Bible invites us to pray. "Let us, therefore, come boldly to the throne of grace, that we may obtain mercy and find grace to help in time of need" (Hebrews 4:16 NKJV).

Hilgemann (2018) writes, "Prayer is how we talk to God. When we pray, God listens. God is like an amazing Father who enjoys giving good gifts to His children (Luke 11:9–13). We should persevere in our prayers until the Lord answers (Luke 18:1–8), but we must have faith in our petition in order for it to be effective (Matthew 21:22)." Hilgemann (2018) also affirms that Jesus frequently sought to get away from the crowds to pray in solitude and quietness (Matthew 14:23; Luke 5:16, 6:12; Mark 1:35).[19]

Today, like Jesus, we should regularly withdraw for time alone with God in prayer. That can mean taking a break from our electronic devices from time to time to listen to God instead of human opinions.

White affirms:

> The human heart longs for sympathy in suffering. This longing Christ felt to the very depths of His being. In the supreme agony of His soul, He came to His disciples with a yearning desire to hear some words of comfort from those whom He had so often blessed and comforted and shielded in sorrow and distress. The One who had always had words of sympathy for them was now suffering superhuman agony, and He longed to know that they were praying for Him and themselves.[20]

She writes:

> It would be well to spend a thoughtful hour each day reviewing the life of Christ from the manger to Calvary. We should take it point by point and let the imagination vividly grasp each scene, especially the closing ones of His earthly life. By thus contemplating His teachings and sufferings, and the infinite sacrifice made by Him for the redemption of the race, we may strengthen our faith, quicken our love, and become more deeply imbued with the spirit which sustained our Savior.[21]

Lynn (2014) writes that the prayers of the apostle Paul primarily dealt with spiritual issues (Ephesians 1:16–19, 3:14–19; Philippians 1:9–11; Colossians 1:9–12), but they specifically pray that followers of Christ will grow in godliness. Failure to pray for living peaceful, quiet, godly, and dignified lives (1 Timothy 2:1–2) has resulted in shallow prayers and weak Christians.

Hull (2007) affirms that a disciple must commit to prayer.

Ask whatever you wish, and it will be given you (John 15:7).

Hull (2007) notes, "A disciple who remains in Christ and understands His Word knows what and how to pray. He knows what to ask for and how to get it. He understands what not to ask for as well. The above verse does not give disciples carte blanche; it must be balanced with many other comments on prayer. Additional qualifications for answered prayer include commandment-keeping (see 1 John 3:22) and praying according to the will of God (see 1 John 5:14–15)."[22]

He continues:

> The disciple is a person of informed and authoritative prayer. Communication with God forms the basis of remaining and the root of living as a disciple. God talks to me through the Scriptures. I talk back to Him through prayer. Getting to know God, in some respects, is like getting to know any person. There is conversation, sharing of lives, the interchange of ideas and opinions. Talking to God is as vital as God talking to us. The disciple learns to talk to God by listening to what God has already said. Prayer responds to what God has already said. Remaining in Christ requires both God's Word and prayer.[23]

Jesus says, "And I tell you, ask … seek … and knock" (Luke 11:9 NKJV). The Bible also tells us that Jesus "told them a parable to the effect that they ought always to pray" (Luke 18:1 NKJV).

White writes:

> As activity increases and men become successful in doing any work for God, there is a danger of trusting to human plans and methods. There is a tendency to pray less and to have less faith. Like the disciples, we are in danger of losing sight of our dependence on God and seeking to make a savior of our activity. We need to look constantly to Jesus, realizing that it is His power that does the work. While we are to labor earnestly for the salvation of the lost, we must also take time for meditation, prayer, and the study of the Word of God. Only the work accomplished with much prayer, and sanctified by the merit of Christ, will, in the end, prove to have been efficient for good.[24]

Hull mentions, "Prayer was the primary tool for recruiting workers to fill the vacant workforce."[25]

Intercessory Prayer

When considering the Bible, we can see that all the great men and women of God were people who practiced intercessory prayer. We all have challenges, yet we must pray for ourselves, as well as for others. Here also, we have to follow Jesus. He is an intercessory Savior. The disciple will therefore also practice intercessory prayer.

> Therefore, I exhort first of all that supplications, prayers, intercessions, and giving of thanks be made for all men, for kings and all who are in authority, that we may lead a quiet and peaceable life in all godliness and reverence. For this is good and acceptable in the sight of God our Savior (1 Timothy 2:1–9 NKJV).

Paul begins this thought by saying, "First of all." That means prayers for others should not be the last on our list. It's a priority to pray for others, those who are in faith, and those who do not believe in Jesus. This is good before God.

Bullón (2017) affirms that we need praying disciples. If we look at the life of the church and the apostles in the first and second centuries, we notice that they learned from the Master. Of course, they prayed for their own material and spiritual needs, but we find them more often praying for others, even for their despised rulers. The life of the early church was a life of constant prayer for other people. And what was the result? The church grew amazingly.

S. Joseph Kidder (2015) says that prayer should permeate all of our efforts to evangelize. Make it your habit, your practice, to pray for your neighbors, family members, coworkers, and acquaintances in the community.

Bullón (2017) mentions that there is no point in running after people if you do not start with prayer. Pray every day for the people you want to lead to Jesus. Intercessory prayer, in addition to helping the person for whom you pray, is right for you. The adverse circumstances that Job faced changed when he began to pray for his friends.

> After Job had prayed for his friends, the Lord restored his fortunes and gave him twice as much as he had before (Job 42:10 NKJV).

Bullón (2017) writes of Daniel's example in Daniel 9, in which we find an intercessory prayer. If you read the entire prayer, you will notice that at no time does Daniel ask for himself. His prayer is for the people of Israel.

> Now, therefore, our God, hear the prayer of Your servant, and his supplications, and for the Lord's sake cause Your face to shine on Your sanctuary, which is desolate. O my God, incline Your ear and hear; open Your eyes and see our desolations, and the city which is called by Your name; for we do not present our supplications before You because of our righteous deeds, but because of Your great mercies (Daniel 9:17–18 NKJV).

Bullón adds that conversion is the work of the Holy Spirit. Therefore, pray, pray, and pray. Do not grow weary from praying. Although progress may seem to elude you, the Spirit of God is working invisibly, and when you least expect it, you will be surprised. Bullón (2017) further writes that there is a need to find a prayer partner, and together, pray for your friends. God will answer from heaven, and they will become new disciples. Jesus taught His disciples to work this way. No one fulfilled the mission alone.

Fasting

Whitney (2014) writes about fasting in these terms: Personal fasting is found in Matthew 6:16–18 when Jesus says we should fast in a way so as not to be noticed by others. Corporative fasts are found in Joel 2:15–16: "Blow the trumpet in Zion, consecrate a fast, call a sacred assembly; gather the people" (NKJV).

In the New Testament, we can see that the congregation of the church at Antioch was fasting together (Acts 13:1–3). We also see the church in

Galatia fasting (Acts 14:21–23). This was done "in every church" (Acts 14:23 NJKV).

White declares, "When Peter also was imprisoned, the entire church engaged in fasting and prayer."[26]

According to Whitney, "God established one regular fast in the old covenant. Each year, every Jew was to fast on the Day of Atonement (see Leviticus 16:29–31)."[27] Today, Jesus expects His followers to fast. Notice Jesus's words at the beginning of Matthew 6:16: "However, when you fast…" By giving us instructions on what to do and what not to do when we fast, Jesus assumes that we will fast.

Moreover, there is nothing here or elsewhere in scripture indicating that we no longer need to fast. We know that Christians in the book of Acts fasted (see 9:9; 13:2; 14:23). Paul exhorts us to pray and fast: "Do not deprive one another except with consent for a time, that you may give yourselves to fasting and prayer; and come together again so that Satan does not tempt you because of your lack of self-control" (1 Corinthians 7:5 NKJV). In fact, Paul fasted a lot: "in weariness and toil, in sleeplessness often, in hunger and thirst, in fastings often, in cold and nakedness" (2 Corinthians 11:27 NKJV).

Whitney writes:

> In the scriptures, we find examples of fasts that lasted one day or part of a day (see Judges 20:26; 1 Samuel 7:6; 2 Samuel 1:12, 3:35; Nehemiah 9:1; Jeremiah 36:6), a one-night fast (see Daniel 6:18–24), three-day fasts (see Esther 4:16; Acts 9:9), seven-day fasts (see 1 Samuel 31:13; 2 Samuel 12:16–23), a fourteen-day fast (see Acts 27:33–34), a twenty-one-day fast (see Daniel 10:3–13), forty-day fasts (see

Deuteronomy 9:9; 1 Kings 19:8; Matthew 4:2), and fasts of unspecified lengths (see Matthew 9:14; Luke 2:37; Acts 13:2, 14:23). Strictly speaking, abstinence from one meal for spiritual purposes constitutes a fast. So, the length of your fast is up to you and the leadership of the Holy Spirit.[28]

Fasting Must Have a Goal

There's more to a biblical fast than merely abstaining from food. Without a spiritual purpose for your fast, it's just a fast for weight loss.

You can fast to strengthen your prayer life, to seek God's guidance, to heal, to seek deliverance and protection, to overcome temptation, or to seek spiritual growth.

White makes the following statements:

> There is a need for fasting, humiliation, and prayer over our decaying zeal and languishing spirituality.[29]

> We need to humble ourselves before the Lord, with fasting and prayer, and to meditate much upon His word, especially upon the scenes of the judgment.

We need to humble ourselves before the Lord, with fasting and prayer, and to meditate much upon His word, especially upon the scenes of the judgment. We should now seek a deep and living experience in the things of God. We have not a moment to lose. Events of vital importance are taking place around us; we are on Satan's enchanted ground. Sleep not, sentinels of God; the foe is lurking near, ready at any moment, should you become lax and drowsy, to spring upon you and make you his prey.[30]

The true fasting which should be recommended to all is abstinence from every stimulating kind of food, and the proper use of wholesome, simple food, which God has provided in abundance. Men need to think less about what they shall eat and drink, of temporal food, and much more concerning the food from heaven that will give tone and vitality to the whole religious experience.[31]

For certain things, fasting and prayer are recommended and appropriate. In the hand of God, they are a means of cleansing the heart and promoting a receptive frame of mind. We obtain answers to our prayers because we humble our souls before God.[32]

Talk less; much precious time is lost in a talk that brings no light. Let brethren unite in fasting and prayer for the wisdom that God has promised to supply liberally.[33]

To succeed in such a conflict, they must come to work in a different spirit. Their faith must be strengthened by fervent prayer and fasting, and humiliation of heart.[34]

I think that you have erred in fasting for two days. God did not require it of you. I beg of you to be cautious and eat freely good, wholesome food twice a day. You will surely decrease in strength, and your mind becomes unbalanced unless you change your course of the abstemious diet.[35]

Whitney (2014) adds, "Fasting is when we hunger for God—for a fresh encounter with God, for God to answer a prayer, for God to save someone, for God to work powerfully in our church, for God to guide us or protect us—more than we hunger for the food God made for us to live on. God once rebuked the Jews, not for their failure to fast but for fasting without a God-centered hunger."

Worship

The Bible orders us to worship God. The disciple puts heavy emphasis on his or her time of worship. In 1 Chronicles 16:29, we read, "Give to the Lord the glory due His name; Bring an offering, and come before Him. Oh, worship the Lord in the beauty of holiness!" (NKJV).

Many believers have made the word "worship" synonymous with singing, but it is much more than that.

Hilgemann writes, "Whether gathered together at church or alone in our rooms, when we think about the greatness of God, we will do only one thing—worship Him."[36]

Whitney (2014) writes that we may also consider worship a discipline that must be cultivated. That will help disciples to remain healthy and grow.

White affirms, "To praise God in fullness and sincerity of heart is as much a duty as is prayer."[37]

Kidder (2015) writes that if anything is worth doing well, it is the worship of our glorious God. We can expect to see changes in worship only with prayer and the work of the Holy Spirit. It is by intentional planning, practice, and communication that we will be able to provide a worship service that honors God while edifying and uplifting members and guests.

Kevin Brosius (2017) mentions that "In 2 Corinthians 3:17–18, Paul declares that it is the Holy Spirit who does the transformative work in the life of believers. Human programs and even discipleship strategy is not what changes lives—only God can work in hearts."

Whitney (2014) asks if you will commit yourself to the discipline of daily worship.

> "If you will not worship God seven days a week," said A. W. Tozer, "you do not worship Him on one day a week." Let's not fool ourselves. True worship, as a once-a-week event, does not exist.[38]

As true disciples, we can't expect our worship to go smoothly like a river on the Sabbath Day if we do not worship God at home every day.

Whitney (2014) affirms, "Jesus Himself reemphasized and obeyed the Old Testament command, 'Thou shalt worship the Lord thy God, and him only shalt thou serve.' [Matthew 4:10] It is the duty (and privilege) of all people to worship their Creator. 'Oh come, let us worship and bow down,' says Psalm 95:6, 'let us kneel before the LORD, our Maker!' God clearly expects us to worship. It's our purpose! Godliness without the worship of God is unthinkable." [39]

In Revelation 4:8, we read of four creatures around the throne who worship God without ceasing:

The four living creatures, each having six wings, were full of eyes around and within. And they do not rest day or night, saying:

> "Holy, holy, holy,
>
> Lord God Almighty,
>
> Who was and is and is to come!" (NKJV)

Isaiah 6:1–4 shows us a partial scene of heavenly worship:

In the year that King Uzziah died, I saw the Lord sitting on a throne, high and lifted up, and the train of His robe filled the temple. Above it stood seraphim; each one had six wings: with two he covered his face, with two he covered his feet, and with two he flew. And one cried to another and said:

"Holy, holy, holy is the Lord of hosts;

The whole earth is full of His glory!"

And the posts of the door were shaken by the voice of him who cried out, and the house was filled with smoke. (NKJV)

Hebrews 12:28 invites us to worship God acceptably "with reverence and godly fear" (NKJV). Hawkins, Kinnaman, and Matlock (2019) state, "Worshipping God and experiencing His presence emerge over and over are key priorities for resilient disciples."[40]

Stewardship

The Bible says, "It is more blessed to give than to receive" (Acts 20:35 NKJV).

Generosity is about more than just giving. It's changing the way you think about and manage your resources.

"There is one who scatters, yet increases more;

And there is one who withholds more than is right,

But it leads to poverty" (Proverbs 11:24 NKJV).

Ecclesiastes 5:10 warns against the love of money because it will never satisfy. But the reason we should be generous is that nothing we own belongs to us. Everything we have belongs to God (Psalm 24:1). We are just managing God's resources.

Jesus often taught about money and possessions. He warned, "Take heed and beware of covetousness, for one's life does not consist in the abundance of the things he possesses" (Luke 12:15 NKJV). Instead, we should store our treasures in heaven because our hearts follow our treasure (Matthew 6:19–21). If we are not careful, the cares of these riches will creep into our lives and keep us from God.

So, Jesus asks, "For what profit is it to a man if he gains the whole world, and loses his own soul? Or what will a man give in exchange for his soul?" (Matthew 16:26 NKJV). Put simply, "You cannot serve God and mammon" (Matthew 6:24 NKJV).

The problem is not the riches; it's our attitude toward money. We need to learn to be content, no matter how much money we have (1 Timothy 6:6). Paul teaches the rich to "be rich in good works, ready to give, willing to share" (1 Timothy 6:17 NKJV). Plus, giving must be done with the right attitude because "God loves a cheerful giver" (2 Corinthians 9:7 NKJV).

Hilgemann mentions, "While most Americans today spend more than they make, those who practice generosity must discipline themselves to live with less. That frees more of our time, money, and possessions to be given back to God."[41]

White says:

> Those who are truly converted are called to do a work that requires money and consecration. The obligations which bind us to place our names on the church roll hold us responsible

to work for God to the utmost of our ability. He calls for undivided service for the entire devotion of heart, soul, mind, and strength. Christ has brought us into church capacity that he may engage and engross all our capabilities in devoted service for the salvation of others. Anything short of this is opposition to work. There are only two places in the universe where we can deposit our treasures—in God's storehouse or Satan's. All that is not devoted to God's service is counted on Satan's side and goes to strengthen his cause.[42]

> "Every sacrifice that is made in His ministry would be recompensed according to 'the exceeding riches of His grace.'"

White writes, "Every sacrifice that is made in His ministry would be recompensed according to 'the exceeding riches of His grace' (Ephesians 2:7 NKJV)."[43]

White says, "The use of Peter's boat for the work of the gospel was richly repaid. He who is 'rich unto all that call upon Him' has said, 'Give, and it will be given to you: good measure, pressed down, shaken together, and running over' (Romans 10:12; Luke 6:38 NKJV)."[44] She writes:

Even now, all created things declare the glory of His excellence. There is nothing, save the selfish heart of man, that lives unto itself. No bird cleaves the air, no animal moves upon

> There is nothing, save the selfish heart of man, that lives unto itself.

the ground but that it ministers to some other life. There is no leaf of the forest or lowly blade of grass that does not have its ministry. Every tree and shrub and leaf pours forth that element of life without which neither man nor animal could live, and man and animal, in turn, minister to the life of tree and shrub and leaf.[45]

White adds, "The call to place all on the altar of service comes to each one."[46]

In Ephesians 5:15–16, Paul said, "See then that you walk circumspectly, not as fools but as wise, redeeming the time because the days are evil" (NKJV). Paul may have exhorted the Christians at Ephesus to make the most of their time because he and/or the Ephesians were experiencing persecution or opposition (such as in Acts 19:23–20:1). In any case, we too need to wisely use every moment because "the days are evil" still.

We also have to understand the disciplined use of money. God owns everything you own. In 1 Corinthians 10:26, Paul quoted Psalm 24:1, which reads, "The earth is the Lord's, and all its fullness, the world and those who dwell therein" (NKJV). God owns everything, including everything you possess, because He created everything. "All the earth is Mine," the Lord said in Exodus 19:5 (NKJV). He declared it again in Job 41:11: "Everything under heaven is Mine" (NKJV).

Paul said, "If anyone does not provide for his own, and especially for those of his household, he has denied the faith and is worse than an unbeliever" (1 Timothy 5:8 NKJV).

Whitney writes, "We own nothing. God owns everything, and we are His managers. For most of us, the house we now call 'my house' was called 'my house' by someone else a few years ago. And a few years from now, someone else will call it 'my house.'"[47]

Giving is an act of worship. In Philippians 4:18, the apostle Paul thanked the Christians in the Grecian city of Philippi for the financial gift they gave to support his missionary ministry; he wrote, "Indeed I have all and abound. I am full, having received from Epaphroditus the things sent from you, a sweet-smelling aroma, an acceptable sacrifice, well-pleasing to God" (NKJV).

God said in Deuteronomy 16:16, "They shall not appear before the Lord empty-handed" (NKJV). Whitney writes that "Giving should be sacrificial and generous. The widow, whom Jesus commended, illustrates the fact that giving to God is not just for those who, as the world would put it, can 'afford it.' The apostle Paul gave another such illustration in 2 Corinthians 8:1–5 when he told of how the poor Christians in Macedonia sacrificed to give generously."[48]

Giving reflects spiritual trustworthiness. Jesus revealed this startling insight into the ways of God's kingdom in Luke 16:10–13 when He said we must give willingly, thankfully, and cheerfully.

Giving should be planned and systematic. Notice how the apostle Paul directs the Christians to give: "Now concerning the collection for the saints, as I have given orders to the churches of Galatia, so you must do also: On the first day of the week let each one of you lay something aside, storing up as he may prosper, that there be no collections when I come" (1 Corinthians 16:1–2 NKJV). This "collection for the saints" was a special offering for the poor Christians suffering in Jerusalem because of a famine.

Evangelism and Witnessing

Disciple-making is a cornerstone of the church. In Acts 5:42, Luke wrote, "And daily in the temple, and in every house, they did not cease teaching and preaching Jesus as the Christ" (NKJV). The first disciples were committed daily to talking about Jesus, sharing the gospel and teaching others how to follow Jesus. It was a daily discipline. Talking about Jesus every day is the duty of every disciple. It's not only the job of some religious people.

We can evangelize according to our talents. Every disciple has received from the Lord one or many talents. In Matthew 25:14–29, Jesus expects every one of His disciples to do something to advance His kingdom, for one day, we will account to God.

Some can evangelize easily through the internet. The internet has changed human behavior all over the globe. Haigh, Russell, and Dutton (2015) retrace the beginning of the internet from the 1960s, with the creation of the ARPANET.[49] In the 1990s, the Institutionalization of Internet Governance laid down basic policies to guide the progress of the field.[50] Statistics indicate that more than 3.8 billion people use the internet. In this digital world, technological innovations are changing everything in our culture and according to Moore's law, there is no coming back.[51] The digital tools of the internet can be a powerful means of creating disciples.

Social media can be used in a very effective way to spread the Word. When well-controlled, Facebook, Twitter, LinkedIn, WhatsApp, Instagram, Tumblr, Tik Tok, etc., can be powerful tools to make disciples. These days, the opportunities are endless. The use of podcasts can be phenomenal as a means to touch people for Christ as well.

Nevertheless, the internet will never replace the personal touch. We must talk to people about what Jesus has done in our personal lives. Nobody can deny our personal experience with Jesus, and every disciple has a unique story to tell others about Jesus.

In the article "The Art of Persuasion Hasn't Changed in 2,000 Years," Carmine Gallo presents five rhetorical devices that can help when we share our story. Aristotle identified them two thousand years ago, and masters of persuasion still use them today: (1) ethos or character, (2) logos or reason, (3) pathos or emotion, (4) metaphor, and (5) brevity.[52]

Conclusion

It might be difficult to practice the spiritual disciplines we have discussed in this chapter, but if you ask God to help you, He will give His Spirit to lead you. After a time, you will form new spiritual habits. These spiritual disciplines will help you in your walk with God.

Personal Application

Today, I realize why my spiritual life used to be so weak. I ask God to forgive my spiritual negligence. I want to follow Jesus in His spiritual disciplines. I want to be more serious about eternal life. I want to take time to read and meditate on the Bible daily. I want to set aside certain days to fast.

Suggested Prayers

1. Jesus, by Your grace, help me to practice spiritual disciplines so I can remain a faithful disciple.

2. O God, do not let me fall into formalism or legalism when I practice spiritual disciplines. Let me be true and sincere in my spiritual life.

3. Jesus, help me to persevere in the practice of spiritual disciplines, as You did until the cross.

CHAPTER 5

---◆ ◆ ◆---

CHOSEN TO DEVELOP A DISCIPLESHIP STRATEGY

"Jesus poured His life into a few disciples and taught them to make other disciples. Seventeen times we find Jesus with the masses, but forty-six times we see Him with His disciples."

—Dann Spader

As I was writing this book, I had an experience that I'd never had before. One night, I had a dream. I saw Jesus's face in a picture frame. The more I stared at Him, the more I saw glory on His face. A few seconds later, the following text appeared: "'Not by might nor by power, but by My Spirit,' says the Lord of hosts" (Zechariah 4:6 NKJV). This dream heavily impacted my life. No human words can express how I feel. This experience profoundly changed my perspective on the text from Zechariah. I experienced how loving and gracious Jesus is. Even when we do not deserve it, He shows us His grace and His mercy. I realized that no matter the circumstances I face in life, the solution will come through the Holy Spirit.

Discipleship is all about Jesus. To be a disciple is to continually look at Jesus. All is possible, only through the Holy Spirit.

Pastors and local church leaders are very busy. It may be hard for them to stay focused on their primary mission—making disciples. It is easy for them to lose focus amid so many challenges, demands, and programs. That is why they need to go outside their regimens from time to time to evaluate their ministries and to hear from the Lord, to lead the church God's way through the Holy Spirit. God longs to reveal Himself more and more to every one of His children. The spiritual leaders are God's instruments to bring His people closer to Him in an unwavering relationship.

Pastor Dave E. Cole writes:

> I recommend leaders take a spiritual retreat each year to get away from all the voices and learn to hear Jesus's voice. Pastors or local church leaders will have difficulty listening to Jesus's voice unless they periodically unplug from all of their electrical devices and get away with just Jesus and His Word. Many voices daily bombard leaders, trying to buy for their time and focus. Jesus's voice is outward-focused. Like a shepherd, He is not content until all His sheep are saved.[1]

Bullón writes that "the primary work of the minister is not to bring people to Christ. That work, in God's plan, must be performed by every believer."[2]

White declares:

> In laboring where there are already some in the faith, the minister should at first seek not so much to convert unbelievers, as to train the church members for acceptable cooperation. Let him labor for them individually, endeavoring to arouse them to seek for a deeper experience themselves. When they are prepared to sustain the minister by their prayers and labors, greater success will attend his efforts.[3]

White declares, "Preaching is a small part of the work to be done for the salvation of souls. God's Spirit convicts sinners of the truth and places them in the arms of the church. The ministers may do their part, but they can never perform the work that the church should do."[4]

She also writes:

> Wherever a church is established, all the members should engage actively in missionary work. They should visit every family in the neighborhood and know their spiritual condition."[5] She adds, "The real character of the church is measured, not by the high profession she makes, not by the names enrolled upon the church book, but by what she is doing for the Master, by the number of her persevering, faithful workers. Personal interest and vigilant, an individual effort will accomplish more for the cause of Christ than can be wrought by sermons or creeds.[6]

Onyinah (2017) writes about the cycle of the Great Commission in Matthew 28:19–20, describing critical components of the discipling cycle for every congregation. The process starts with disciples gaining the attention of others to Christ, baptizing them (integrating them into the local church), and teaching them to obey Christ's commandments.

White declares, "It is a fatal mistake to suppose that the work of soul-saving depends alone upon the ministry."[7] She adds, "It is training, education, that is needed. Those who labor in visiting the churches should give the brethren and sisters instruction in practical methods of doing missionary work."[8]

She writes, "There should be no delay in this well-planned effort to educate the church members."[9] She mentions that "There is need of Nehemiah in the church today, —not men who can pray and preach only, but men whose prayers and sermons are braced with firm and eager purpose."[10]

Write further says that "God expects His church to discipline and fit its members for the work of enlightening the world."[11] She says, "The greatest help that can be given to our people is to teach them to work for God, and to depend on Him, not on the ministers."[12]

She adds, "It is by education and practice that persons are to be qualified to meet any emergency which may arise, and wise planning is needed to place each one in his proper sphere, that he may obtain an experience that will fit him to bear responsibility."[13]

White also writes: "The best help that ministers can give the members of our churches is not sermonizing but planning work for them."[14] She says, "The Lord desires us to obtain all the education possible, with the object in view of imparting our knowledge to others"[15] and affirms, "In proportion to the enthusiasm and perseverance with which the work is carried forward, will be the success given."[16]

We all know that we must lead by example. If the pastor or the church leader is not adequately trained as a disciple of Jesus or does not believe in discipleship, it will be tough for the church to excel in discipleship and to follow Jesus's orders. The river cannot rise above its source.

Hull (2007) writes that most plans do not succeed because the pastor is not trained as a disciple. How can someone motivate people to make disciples without practicing the very things he or she advocates?

> Pastors and local church leaders are called on to reach all generations.

Pastors and local church leaders are called on to reach all generations. The Great Commission is for all nations. All generations are included in "all nations," so we must make plans to reach all generations in our local churches: Baby Boomers (1946–1964), Generation X (1965–1976), Millennials (1977–1995), Generation Z or iGeneration (1996–2014), and Generation Alpha (the children of Millennials).

Hull makes note of the researcher George Barna, who, after studying the five best models of discipleship, came to the following conclusion regarding how a church can succeed in discipleship. For the church to move forward, it must return to making disciples. Here is how that would look:

- The senior pastor is an irrepressible advocate of discipleship.
- Church members participate in a focused, demanding discipleship process.
- All ministries are intimately tied to discipleship outcomes.
- The number of programs is minimized to focus the church on discipleship.
- All teaching of the church is substantively coordinated.

- The church's mission statement serves as a practical tool for identifying ministry outcomes.[17]

The church must have a discipleship cycle program. Hull (2007) writes that a church could build a plan for discipleship by identifying how the individual will grow in five specific areas: (1) Bible knowledge, (2) practical ministry skills, (3) outreach, (4) prayer, and (5) accountability. The church can run a discipleship program over a six-month cycle, divided into six modules per year, or a one- or three-year cycle divided into three or six modules per year.

In our minds, we must already anticipate the result: we plan to grow disciples. Here again, it is time to follow Jesus. Eims and Coleman (2009) explain that Jesus was not seeking to fascinate the crowd but to build a kingdom. That implies that He wanted people who could lead the multitudes.

Bullón (2017) writes that God's ideal for His church is a glorious church, without wrinkle and without blemish, like a bride dressed in white, waiting for her groom—an authentic church, without formalities, not merely concerned with appearances.

> Obey them not only to win their favor when their eye is on you but as slaves of Christ, doing the will of God from your heart. Serve wholeheartedly, as if you were serving the Lord, not people (Ephesians 6:6–7 KJV).

But what does Paul mean when he refers to a glorious church? Obviously, it is glorious because it reflects the glory of God.

White mentions that "the Lord wants us to make the very best and highest use that is possible of the talents that He has given us."[18]

Hull (2007) argues that making a disciple has three components. The first is deliverance, which is achieved via evangelism when a person is converted and baptized. The second is development—what most people call discipleship or personal growth—in which a person is grounded in the faith. That is continuous and lifelong, essential for the care of the soul. The third component is deployment; at that time, the grounded disciple is appointed to a mission in his or her community. A church or pastor or church leader engaged in making disciples should be concentrated on this process as the first priority.

Hull writes:

> My advice to all pastors is simply to rearrange your life around the practices of Jesus. Look at His life filled with the press of the crowd, the hatred of religious leaders, and the dullness of His disciples. How did He handle it? He prayed alone, and He prayed at special times of pressure and decision. He lived a life focused on others, a life that was based on humility and sacrifice powered by love.[19]

Hull (2007) argues that the difficulty for pastors is to be a disciple first, seeking God every day and practicing the spiritual disciplines He advocates. That, however, is becoming harder to do. He adds, "The church is for training the saints. Once they are equipped, they become healthy disciples who will penetrate every segment of society with both the words and the works of the gospel."

Evangelism or Discipleship

Hull (2010) affirms that because the pastoral task is multidimensional and multileveled, the disciple-making pastor's responsibility is to manage various levels of people's development.

Babcock (2002) mentions that to produce a disciple-making church, we should give particular focus to the ministry of all new believers. Consequently, in most small groups, there should be a proper program of small groups to encourage one-on-one ministry.

In this work of discipleship, if we follow Jesus's voice, there is no failure.

White declares, "Workers for Christ are never to think, much less to speak, of failure in their work. The Lord Jesus is our efficiency in all things; His Spirit is to be our inspiration, and as we place ourselves in His hands to be channels of light, our means of doing good will never be exhausted."[20]

Petrie et al., in the article "Developing a Discipleship Measurement Tool," present at least three essential discipleship tools:

1. The Summit Point Discipleship Assessment Test (Styron 2004:58) suggests seven key areas of growth that can be measured: willingness to follow and obey Christ, identification with Christ, willingness to grow and learn, total surrender, ongoing relationship with Christ, growing in Christ-like character and evangelism, and victory over sin.

2. The Together Growing Fruitful Disciples (TGFD) framework and online assessment tool is the result of a collaborative initiative between the General Conference

of Seventh-day Adventists and Andrews University. It contains four central pillars: connecting (with God, self, family, church, and others); understanding (spiritual growth, nature of God, sin, and suffering, redemption, restoration); equipping (being discipled and discipling others in connecting understanding and ministering); and ministering (personal vocation, friendships, community service, stewardship, evangelism).

3. The Christian Life Profile Assessment Tool (Frazee 2005:6) is a discipleship kit designed to enable churches to assess beliefs, practices, and attitudes within thirty key competencies.21

1. Assess the discipleship status of your church

The pastor or local church leader must make an assessment of the discipleship status in his or her church. Brown (2012) mentions, "There is a notable hole between where the church is and where it is supposed to be. Interpreting this deficit is a crucial step that cannot be overlooked. If the church does not recognize or embrace the reality of the problem, the transformation most likely will not occur."

Wegner and Magruder (2012) write that every believer should be a reproducing follower of Jesus, and every church should be a reproducing church. If we understand that reproduction is God's will for all of us, then we will develop our systems accordingly.

White declares, "Every church should be a training school for Christian workers. Its members should be taught how to give Bible readings, how to conduct and teach Sabbath-school classes, how to best help the poor and care for the sick, and how to work for the unconverted."[22]

> Every church should be a training school for Christian workers.

2. Be intentional

Making disciples is a serious business in God's church. We must be intentional in this regard. We cannot do this by accident or circumstantially.

Hélène Thomas explains:

After baptism, the new convert penetrates the regular membership of the church, and the enthusiasm spent on the new convert usually comes to an abrupt end. The new members are often left to navigate the new life by themselves. The result is that not many church friends are made, vital spiritual habits are not developed, and backsliding is common. Sadly, many new members eventually leave the church, walking out the proverbial back door with little notice. Without an

> Without an intentional process of discipleship, even the new members who continue to attend church services often develop a complacent habit of doing little more than warming the pew each week.

intentional process of discipleship, even the new members who continue to attend church services often develop a complacent habit of doing little more than warming the pew each week.[23]

Hull (2010) writes, "The first church had the intentional strategy of making disciples, as described in Acts 2:42–47. Guided by Acts 1:8, the twelve apostles must have planned to send out many disciples. A reproductive congregation led to believers who reproduced the same practices wherever they went. They would start churches by preaching and would organize converts into small groups." He adds, "The characteristics of disciple-making are intentional, measurable, clearly communicated ministry. … Many forces militate against disciple-making. In theory, disciple-making is popular because it promises a quality product that honors God. In practice, however, it requires time, dedication, and patience that pastors living in American culture find difficult."

Onyinah (2017) mentions that disciples have to create an intentional friendship to bring the person to what they desire a disciple to be. Thus, friendship is critical in disciple-making.

> The method Jesus used to train disciples was an intentional relational discipleship.

Harrington (2017) declares that the method Jesus used to train disciples was an intentional relational discipleship. Many church leaders are not intentional in creating discipleship in their churches. Chisholm (2016) affirms that, unfortunately, the process of discipleship in many churches is informal and unintentional.

Thomas affirms that those who are serious about fulfilling the command to "Go … and make disciples" (Matthew 28:19 NKJV) cannot think that their work is done after baptism: "New members need to be intentionally mentored until they form healthy habits of prayer, Bible study, family worship, and regular attendance at Sabbath school, church, and prayer meetings. They need to be intentionally befriended by multiple members of the church. They need ongoing instruction to develop an even deeper love and understanding of the Seventh-day Adventist message. As members of the remnant church, they need to be trained to share the truth with others through personal witnessing."[24]

Hull (2007) writes, "The bare bones of obedience is the intentional effort to define a disciple, and then to produce disciples through various vehicles of the church."[25]

3. Have a vision for multiplication, not addition

Hull (2007) affirms that one of the fundamentals of obedience is a commitment to multiplication. The evidence of such commitment can be seen in the selection of those with leadership ability to be trained as disciple-makers. He says, "Good leaders know how to frame an issue. Look at how Jesus framed the need for multiplication of ministry. Compassion for unmet need was the prime motive. … The objective for multiplication was extending God's love and care on a wider basis through a wider workforce. Prayer was the primary tool for recruiting workers to fill the vacant workforce."[26]

Hull (2007) declares, "The successful completion of the Great Commission depends on multiplication. Disciple-making results in reproduction; the result of reproduction among several people is multiplication. Jesus stated the Great Commission the way He did because 'make disciples of all nations' means much more than 'make converts of all nations.' Only healthy disciples reproduce. If the church fails to make disciples, it fails to multiply. If the church fails to multiply, it fails."[27]

Hull adds, "On Paul's first two mission tours, he planted more than fifteen churches. ... Paul's first tour lasted two years and included eight cities. Luke covers the mission in eighty verses (Acts 13:1–14:28). For the early church, this step was multiplication, and for Antioch, it was a reproduction. For Paul and Barnabas, it was formative work: they had to feel their way along and creatively contextualize their principles."[28]

> Then He said to them, "The harvest truly is great, but the laborers are few; therefore, pray the Lord of the harvest to send out laborers into His harvest" (Luke 10:2 NKJV).

Hull (2007) also talks about prayer and multiplication: "We may be perplexed about the multiplication effect of the church. Karl Barth writes, 'Perplexity comes to us simply because we are ministers.' Jesus voiced a simple solution: pray for workers to enter the harvest."[29]

White affirms, "If we would humble ourselves before God, and be kind and courteous and tenderhearted and pitiful, there would be one hundred conversions to the truth where now there is only one."[30]

4. Establish a discipleship system for the church

In this twenty-first century, everywhere we go, we see a system to sustain the growth of any organization. Why is there a lack of systems for discipleship within churches? Lynn (2014) contests that without a system, discipleship cannot be implemented successfully in any church.

> In this twenty-first century, everywhere we go, we see a system to sustain the growth of any organization.

On this issue, Seifert (2013) points out a managerial problem inside our churches. The problem, she says, is that church systems have not enabled followers of Jesus to reproduce and multiply. She adds that while churches may excel in programs and ministries, these programs and ministries are not making disciples of Jesus Christ.[31]

Hull (2010) mentions that "discipling means managing a system in which teaching, training, evangelism, and pastoral care take place. It involves the multidimensional work of the leadership team as they coach the congregation in a variety of ways."[32]

But if we had a system for new converts to become disciples, we would see the difference. They would grow. White says, "Christians who are constantly growing in earnestness, in zeal, in fervor, in love—such Christians never backslide."[33]

Hull (2010) affirms:

The church has the responsibility to provide the clear vision and the vehicles that bring Christians into mature discipleship. Growth and accountability should be part of every Christian's life, for his or her entire life; the need for these doesn't end until one gets transferred to heaven. The key to church-centric discipling is teamwork

> The church has the responsibility to provide the clear vision and the vehicles that bring Christians into mature discipleship.

in a loving environment that maintains the distinctives of mission, training in ministry skills, and accountability. The real evidence of success will be the constant production of reproducing disciples and leaders who become multipliers.

5. Develop a discipleship strategy for the members

In Ephesians 4, the Holy Spirit talks about the way to equip saints, and the necessity of doing so:

> And He Himself gave some to be apostles, some prophets, some evangelists, and some pastors and teachers, for the equipping of the saints for the work of ministry, for the edifying of the body of Christ, till we all come to the unity of the faith and of the knowledge of the Son of God, to a perfect man, to the measure of the stature of the fullness of Christ; that we should no longer be children, tossed to and fro and carried about with every wind of doctrine, by the trickery of men, in the cunning craftiness of deceitful plotting, but, speaking the truth in love, may grow up in all things into Him who is the head—Christ—from whom the whole body, joined and knit together by what every joint supply, according to the effect by which every part does its share, causes growth

of the body for the edifying of itself in love. (Ephesians 4:11–16 NKJV)

Bullón (2015) declares that God distributed gifts to His children "for the equipping of the saints for the work of ministry, for the edifying of the body of Christ" (Ephesians 4:12 NKJV). He adds that "personal witness is not a gift but a spiritual need, such as prayer or Daily Bible study."[34]

Bill Hull and Bobby Harrington (2014) write:

> Gifted leaders are responsible to equip people for their work. The gifted leaders referenced in the text are apostles, prophets, evangelists, pastors, and teachers. All of these roles are needed to match the diversity of gifts that God has given His people. The saints need the apostles' impulse to press forward, the courage and clarity of the prophet, the desire to tell the story of the evangelist, the care and attention of the pastor, and the principles and knowledge of the teacher. "Equip" is a comprehensive word. It means to mend a frayed net, to reset a broken bone, to prepare for athletic competition. We like to describe it as "coaching." Multidimensional gifted leaders are needed to prepare a diverse group of people.[35]

Gifted leaders are responsible to equip people for their work.

White says it is not "the capabilities you now possess or ever will have, that will give you success. It is that which the Lord can do for you. We need to have far less confidence in what man can do and far more confidence in what God can do for every believing soul."[36]

Hull and Harrington (2014) write that equipping the saints "continues until the saints individually and corporately meet the standard of Christlikeness. The standard for stopping the equipping process is 'until we all come to such unity in our faith and knowledge of God's Son that we will be mature in the Lord,

> Equipping the saints "continues until the saints individually and corporately meet the standard of Christlikeness."

measuring up to the full and complete standard of Christ' (Ephesians 4:13 NLT). Equipping the saints never ceases. There are always issues in a saint's life that need strengthening, sins needing to be confessed and lessons to be learned" and add that equipping the saints "addresses the problems of immaturity, disunity, instability, deception, inactivity, shallowness, addiction to desire, and lack of focus."[37]

Seifert (2013) quotes Wheatley (2006) to affirm that today's leaders face a world where continuous change is the norm.[38] All organizations need management and leadership, but leadership is particularly necessary to solve problems that do not have easy answers.[39] Pastors and church leaders are called to lead in a culture of change. They must constantly train the members to help them to stay focused on the mission.

6. Develop a discipleship strategy for leaders

To do the work of discipleship, you need a team. For an effective discipleship program, we need leaders who understand and practice discipleship.

You cannot prepare a true disciple-making leader without bringing him or her to Jesus first. Only in daily fellowship with Christ can the character of Jesus be produced in the person. Leaders themselves do not perceive that they are humble, but those who relate to them do notice that their lives reflect the character of the Master. Paul wrote:

> Let this mind be in you which was also in Christ Jesus, who, being in the form of God, did not consider it robbery to be equal with God, but made Himself of no reputation, taking the form of a bondservant, and coming in the likeness of men. And being found in appearance as a man, He humbled Himself and became obedient to the point of death, even the death of the cross. Therefore, God also has highly exalted Him and given Him the name which is above every name, that at the name of Jesus every knee should bow, of those in heaven, and of those on earth, and of those under the earth, and that every tongue should confess that Jesus Christ is Lord, to the glory of God the Father (Philippians 2:5–11 NKJV).

Murrell and Murrell (2016) declare, "We multiply disciples by teaching them to walk on an increasing path of obedience. We develop and multiply leaders by teaching them to walk on an increasing path of servanthood. The two are closely related." They add that a healthy church follows Jesus's example. "Like a train, it runs on two rails—one is discipleship; the other is developing and multiplying leaders. Neglect either one and the train will tip over."

Robert Kaplan and David Norton (2014) write that modern human resource organizations are expected to guide the development of leaders and to help shape the organization's culture. Although it is difficult to quantify, good leadership and a supportive culture are essential enablers of a successful execution of strategy.

Hull mentions, "Leadership must define *disciple*, develop a method to make disciples, and model before the congregation what a disciple is and how to make one."[40]

Murrell and Murrell (2016) argue that leadership is supposed to be plural. If you are called to lead, then you are called to build a team so you can lead together. In their 2016 book *The Multiplication Challenge*, they write that no one is called to wander around, trying to accomplish God's will alone. Here are some great examples of leading together in the Bible according to Murrell and Murrell:

> **Moses.** Moses was a great leader (maybe the greatest leader in the Old Testament), but he knew better than to attempt to lead alone. He built a team that included his brother and spokesman, Aaron. Team Moses also included a dude named Hur, and a fearless young warrior named Joshua. Moses was a great leader, in part, because he had a great team. As the team leader, Moses took the blame when things went wrong and shared the honor when things went right. After a historic victory over the Amalekites, Moses summarized the battle with these words, "And Joshua overwhelmed Amalek and his people with the sword." (See Exodus 17:8–13.) Moses was secure enough to give credit for the victory to a young, next-generation leader. Are you secure enough to give credit to young leaders? Secure leaders give credit. Insecure leaders hoard credit.
>
> **David.** David was Israel's greatest king ever, but, like Moses, he never led alone. He had his "mighty men," who could shoot an arrow and sling a stone with the right and left hand. David's team was led by an executive committee of three that

was chaired by Jashobeam the Hachmonite. Read that name again, real slow. Jashobeam the Hachmonite, a.k.a. "The Beam." That's a leader's name if I ever heard one. In one famous battle, The Beam killed 300 enemy warriors with his spear, all by himself. If I'm ever in a war, I think I want someone like Jashobeam the Hachmonite on my team. David was a great leader because he surrounded himself with great men.

Daniel. Daniel's team included his best friends, Hananiah, Mishael, and Azariah (a.k.a. Shadrach, Meshach, and Abednego). Daniel knew he would need a team in order to successfully overcome the temptations of Babylon. Ultimately, he and his friends not only endured temptation together, but were recognized by their leaders and peers as ten times better than all the other young men in Babylon. They had hoped that they would be "better together" and they were. (See Daniel 1:11–20.)

Jesus. Even Jesus refused to do ministry alone. He had His twelve, plus a larger team of seventy. If anyone could have done it alone, it would have been Jesus, but He spent three years building a team.

Leadership is supposed to be plural. If you are called to lead, then you are called to build a team so you can lead together. That's a good thing, because all of us will always be better together.[41]

Hull (2007) affirms, "Most churches lose their strength and die when they cease to produce new leaders. The development of an ever-increasing leadership community ensures the church's future. Even though a pastor claims to a disciple by the preaching track, if he fails to form a leadership group, he has copped out. To widely implement and communicate discipling to the church populace, he must also develop leaders. Without this, reproduction does not exist, and multiplication cannot occur."[42]

> Most churches lose their strength and die when they cease to produce new leaders. The development of an ever-increasing leadership community ensures the church's future. Without this, reproduction does not exist, and multiplication cannot occur.

Murrell and Murrell write, "While it's vital for leaders to continually grow in their calling, compassion for people, and communication skills, the most important and foundational aspect of growing like a leader is to grow in character. If our character is growing, everything else needed for effective leadership will grow accordingly."[43]

Babcock (2002) writes that unless present leaders equip others, there will always be a shortage of leaders. Leadership in discipleship is the key to growth.

7. Develop a discipleship strategy for children and youth

Hawkins, Kinnaman, and Matlock (2019) write about the influence of digital media. Young people are the first generation of humans who cannot rely on the earned wisdom of older generations to help them live with these rapid technological developments. Rather than older adults and traditions, many young people prefer to turn to friends and algorithms.

White writes, "We have an army of youth today who can do a lot if they are properly directed and encouraged."[44] She adds, "Every youth who follows Christ's example of faithfulness and obedience in His lowly home might claim those words spoken of Him by the Father through the Holy Spirit, 'Behold! My Servant whom I uphold, My Elect One in whom My soul delights!' (Isaiah 42:1 NKJV)."[45]

White says, "Parents should teach their children the value and right use of time. Teach them that to do something that will honor God and bless humanity is worth striving for. Even in their early years, they can be missionaries for God."[46] She affirms, "The home is the child's first school, and it is here that the foundation should be laid for a life of service."[47]

Lynn (2014) writes that the family unit is deteriorating at a rapid rate, more so than in the past. Many young people are graduating high school and leaving the church in droves. Research indicates that this is due to children not seeing an authentic Christian life manifested in their parents. They think that their parents are hypocrites. They conclude that Christianity "doesn't work." Lynn mentions that the statistic that showed the "point of no return age" of someone coming to Christ, which was previously age eighteen, has now been lowered to ten. Parents must be the primary spiritual equippers of their children. They have to be equipped to know how to do that.

Brosius mentions that in Josh McDowell's book, *The Last Christian Generation*, he declares that "85 percent of kids who come from Christian families do not have a biblical worldview. Most of them are leaving the church between ages eighteen and twenty-four."[48] Harrington and Putman claim, "Fewer than one out of five who claim to be born-again Christians have a worldview of even a few fundamental biblical beliefs."[49]

Harrington and Putman cite David Kinnaman to say, "Most Christians will die without ever sharing their faith with someone, and sixty to eighty percent of young people will leave the church in their twenties."[50]

William F. Cox Jr. and Robert A. Peck (2018) argue that this matter of discipleship is especially crucial for children for at least the following three reasons (see Matthew 18:3, 19:140):

1. Bible text and the educational receptivity of humans reveal that learners are most impressionable and teachable in the early years of life (cf. Lk. 1:41–44; Moll 2014; Tough 2012; Vemy 1981; 2 Tim. 3:15).

2. From a biblical and Jewish historical perspective, children were prepared beforehand for the teen years' onset of adulthood (cf. Barclay 1959; Lk. 2:42–44; Isa. 7:15).

3. The likelihood of becoming a Christian is highest during the school-age years, diminishing significantly after that (Bama 2017; Culbertson 2015).[51]

8. Develop a discipleship strategy for new members

Brown (2012) says that one specific ministry that should be the cornerstone of discipleship is a new members' class. This training is indispensable to the church and vital to the spiritual maturation of new believers. Research demonstrates that new membership classes are the perfect stage at which to communicate the vision of the church and the expectations of congregants.

> Discipleship is the fastest way to multiply leaders.

Waylon B. Moore writes, "Evangelism is the means to making converts and the training ground for developing disciples. When the church exhales disciples, it inhales converts; thus, the church grows. Discipleship is the fastest way to multiply leaders who will expedite both evangelism and discipleship."[52] Babcock affirms, "Discipleship is winning, building, and equipping new believers to the point of their becoming spiritual reproducers."[53]

Green writes that the disciples also practiced this second arm of making disciples. Following the conversion of three thousand people at Pentecost, the disciples engaged new converts by teaching them: "They continued steadfastly in the apostles' doctrine and fellowship, in the breaking of bread, and in prayers" (Acts 2:42 NKJV). Thus, making disciples is a two-step process. It includes evangelizing people so that they express faith in Jesus Christ as well as teaching them to become like Christ.

Hull (2010) declares that this is why new church plants have the most success when the pastor is firmly fixed on principles similar to Paul's and

Barnabas's, builds the church on evangelism, develops the new converts into mature followers of Jesus, and selects leaders from the most promising new Christians.

9. Plan for alignment

Alignment is an element of strategic planning, and we find this principle in the Bible. In the endeavor of discipleship, if there is no alignment in our plans, it will be chaotic. Paul said, "Nevertheless, to the degree that we have already attained, let us walk by the same rule, let us be of the same mind" (Philippians 3:16 NKJV). In Romans 16:17, he wrote, "Now I urge you, brethren, note those who cause divisions and offenses, contrary to the doctrine which you learned, and avoid them" (NKJV).

Paul also said in 1 Corinthians 1:10, "Now I plead with you, brethren, by the name of our Lord Jesus Christ, that you all speak the same thing, and that there be no divisions among you, but that you be perfectly joined together in the same mind and in the same judgment" (NKJV).

White writes, "Angels work harmoniously. Perfect order characterizes all their movements. The more closely we imitate the harmony and order of the angelic host, the more successful will be the efforts of these heavenly agents on our behalf."[54] She adds, "O how Satan would rejoice if he could succeed in his efforts to get in among this people and disorganize the work at a time when the organization is essential and will be the greatest power to keep out spurious uprisings and to refute claims not endorsed by the Word of God!"[55]

Hull (2010) affirms, "Satan uses many subversive, insidious means to divide the church: everything from the elders fighting the trustees to the women's missionary society warring with the kids clubs' leaders to keep the youngsters out of the church kitchen."[56]

Kaplan and Norton write that the main aim in developing human resources "is to ensure their alignment with the enterprise strategy. Leaders must understand the strategy toward which they are mobilizing their organization, and they must create the values that support this strategy. The enterprise value proposition here is to ensure the alignment of leadership and culture with the strategy."[57]

They add, "Strategy is formulated at the top, but it must be executed at the bottom—by machine operators, call center representatives, delivery truck drivers, sales executives, and engineers. If employees don't understand the strategy or are not motivated to achieve it, the enterprise's strategy is bound to fail. Human capital alignment is achieved when employees' goals, training, and incentives become aligned with the business strategy."[58]

Kaplan and Norton also mention that "strategy is explicitly identified as the focal point of the management system" while "alignment is identified as an explicit part of the management process. Executing strategy requires the highest level of integration and teamwork among organizational units and processes. ... Without strong executive leadership, constructive change is not possible."[59]

They mention further that "when no one is held accountable for overall organization alignment, the opportunity to create value through synergy can be missed. Communicate and educate to create intrinsic motivation."[60] They give five key principles for aligning an organization's measurement and management systems for strategizing:

1. Mobilize change through executive leadership.
2. Translate strategy into operational terms.
3. Align the organization to the strategy.
4. Motivate to make strategy everyone's job.
5. Govern to make strategy a continual process.[61]

Alignment is not a one-time event; it's a process.

White declares, "The secret of our success in the work of God is found in the harmonious work of our people."[62] If we want our members to become disciples of Jesus, a strategy is needed. I praise the Lord because if we want to refocus, we already have the strategy in the Great Commission from Matthew 28:18–20. By implementing the strategy for discipleship, you will discover the joy of making disciples again.

Personal Application

I have to do many things differently to keep the fire of discipleship alive in my personal life and in the life of my church. I must develop new habits to be faithful to God's calling.

Suggested Prayers

1. Jesus, help me to keep the alignment of Your church for discipleship.
2. Jesus, let me serve You not by tradition but according to Your will, clearly revealed to me.
3. Jesus, help me to keep the unity of Your church to make disciples.
4. O God! By Your grace, I would like to be a game-changer as a disciple of Jesus.

PART III

WHAT DOES A DISCIPLE DO?

CHAPTER 6

———◆—◆—◆———

CHOSEN TO MAKE DISCIPLES FOR CHRIST

"All who are called to salvation are called to discipleship, no exceptions, no excuses!"
—Bill Hull

One of the churches for which I minister experienced a moment of joy like never before. A sister of the church had been praying for a long time for the conversion of her husband. It was her dream. One Sabbath, the husband came and made the decision to follow Jesus, and after some weeks, he was baptized. I was amazed to see how all the church members were so happy to see this event. Again, I realized that, indeed, there is joy in making disciples. I believe every believer can testify to the joy of seeing someone decide to follow Jesus. Every believer is chosen by Jesus not only to be a disciple but also to make disciples.

Hull (2006) mentions that discipleship is not just a process but a lifestyle. It is not a temporary aspect; it remains permanent throughout the course of our lives. Discipleship isn't for new converts alone; it's a daily call for all Christians during their lives. Discipleship isn't just one program of the church; it is what the church does. It's not just an aspect of the progress of God's kingdom; the presence of earnest disciples is the most significant testimony of God's business on earth.

White writes, "In His wisdom, the Lord brings those who are seeking for truth into touch with fellow beings who know the truth."[1]

A Call for Every Follower of Jesus

White writes:

> The call to give all to the altar of service comes to each one. We are not all asked to serve as Elisha, nor are we all bidden to sell everything we have, but God asks us to give His service the highest priority in our lives, to allow no day to pass without doing something to advance His work on earth. He does not expect the same kind of service from all. One may be called to ministry in a foreign land; another may be asked to give of his means for the support of gospel work. God accepts the offering of each. It is the consecration of life and all its interests that are deemed necessary. Those who make this consecration will hear and obey the call of heaven.[2]

She adds, "God wants us to make the very best and highest use of the talents that He has given us."[3]

White writes, "Every true disciple is born into the kingdom of God as a missionary. He who drinks of the living water becomes a fountain of life. The receiver becomes a giver."[4] She affirms, "God expects personal service

> Every true disciple is born into the kingdom of God as a missionary.

from everyone to whom He has entrusted a knowledge of the truth for this time and that to save souls should be the lifework of everyone who professes Christ."[5]

She writes, "Each one of us has a mission of incredible importance that he cannot neglect or ignore, as the fulfillment of it involves the weal of some soul and the neglect of it the woe of one for whom Christ died."[6]

We cannot leave our tasks to someone else. White writes, "Your duty cannot be shifted upon another. No one but you can do your work. If you withhold your light, someone must be left in darkness through your neglect."[7] She says, "God demands that every soul who knows the truth shall seek to win others to the love of the truth."[8] She adds, "If you are genuinely consecrated, God will, through your instrumentality, bring into the truth others whom He can use as channels to convey light to many that are groping in darkness."[9]

Harrington declares that "the Great Commission could not happen the way Jesus intended until everyday Christians actively participate and stop relying on pastors and church leaders to make disciples."[10]

Bullón (2017) gives practical ways to become personally involved in making disciples. Choose five people you would like to bring to Jesus. Conversion is the work of the Holy Spirit. Therefore, pray, pray, and pray. Do not grow weary from praying. Go where people gather. Learn to love people and to feel compassion for them. He adds that the mission that God entrusted to His church is not just a corporate mission, but includes the participation of every believer. Jesus never imagined His church fulfilling the task with the involvement of only a few members.

Any evangelistic plan that leaves the believer just watching is not His plan. "This is not God's way of working."[11]

Hull (2010) writes, "Every disciple is called to make disciples." He adds that "a commitment to be and make disciples must be the central act of every disciple and every church."

> Make disciples must be the central act of every disciple and every church.

White makes this solemn declaration:

> We can never be saved in indolence and inactivity.

We can never be saved in indolence and inactivity. There is no such thing as a truly converted person living a helpless, useless life. It is not possible for us to drift into heaven. No sluggard can enter there. Those who refuse to co-operate with God on earth would not co-operate with Him in heaven. It would not be safe to take them to heaven.[12]

A Way to Grow Spiritually

The disciple is called to grow beyond his or her expectations. Jesus gives full power to every true disciple. Luke 9:1–2 tells us, "Then He called His twelve disciples together and gave them power and authority over all demons, and to cure diseases. He sent them to preach the kingdom of God and to heal the sick" (NKJV). That is real—the disciple of Jesus has power and authority over all demons.

White writes, "There is no limit to the usefulness of one who, by putting self aside, makes room for the working of the Holy Spirit upon his heart and lives a life wholly consecrated to God."[13] She adds, "The lack of real dignity and Christian refinement in the ranks of Sabbath-keepers is against us as people and makes the truth that we profess unsavory. The work of educating the mind and manners may be carried forward to perfection. If those who profess the truth do not now improve their privileges and opportunities to grow up to the full stature of men and women in Christ Jesus, they will be no honor to the cause of truth, no honor to Christ."[14]

White declares, "The Lord desires us to use every gift we have, and if we do this, we shall have more significant gifts to use. He does not supernaturally endow us with the qualifications we lack, but while we use that which we have, He will work with us to increase and strengthen every faculty. By every wholehearted, earnest sacrifice for the Master's service, our powers will increase."[15]

She declares, "The only way to grow in grace is to be interestedly doing the very work Christ has enjoined upon us to do."[16] She says, "It is the privilege of every soul to make advancement. Those who are connected with Christ will grow in grace and in the knowledge of the Son of God, to the full stature of men and women. If all who claim to believe the truth had made the most of their ability and opportunities to learn and to do, they would have become strong in Christ. Whatever their occupation—whether they were farmers, mechanics, teachers, or pastors—if they had wholly consecrated themselves to God, they would have become efficient workers for the heavenly Master."[17]

She declares, "Affection might be as clear as crystal and beauteous in its purity, yet it may be shallow because it has not been tested. Make Christ first, last, and best in everything. Constantly behold Him, and your love for Him will daily become deeper and stronger as it is submitted to the test of trial. And as your love for Him increases, your love for each other will grow deeper and stronger."[18]

She adds, "Our growth in grace and joy and our usefulness all depend on our oneness with Christ. We grow in grace by spending time with Him, day by day, hour by hour. He not only creates our faith, but He makes it perfect."[19]

White declares:

> God could have reached His object in saving sinners without our aid, but for us to develop a character like Christ's, we must share in His work. In order to enter into His joy—the joy of seeing souls redeemed by His sacrifice—we must participate in His labors for their redemption.[20]

She says, "Those who do nothing in the cause of God will fail to grow in grace and in the knowledge of the truth."[21]

A Work Not without Difficulties

Working for God is not without difficulties, but God makes provision to give you victory at every twist and turn of the fight. White says, "Satan summoned all his forces and, at every step, contested the work of Christ. So

Working for God is not without difficulties, but God makes provision to give you victory at every twist and turn of the fight.

it will be in the great final conflict of the controversy between righteousness and sin. While new life and light and power are descending from on high upon the disciples of Christ, a new life is springing up from beneath and energizing the agencies of Satan."[22]

She adds, "Meditation and prayer would keep us from rushing unbidden into the way of danger, and thus we should be saved from many a defeat."[23] In this battle, we must rely on God's Word and prayer. White mentions that "it was by the word of God that Christ overcame the wicked one."[24]

In their fight, the authors of the New Testament experienced the power of prayer.

> But recall the former days in which, after you were illuminated, you endured a great struggle with sufferings (Hebrews 10:32 NKJV).

> Pray for us; for we are confident that we have a good conscience, in all things desiring to live honorably. But I especially urge you to do this, that I may be restored to you the sooner (Hebrews 13:18 NKJV).

Throughout his ministry, Paul asked others to pray for him. In 1 Thessalonians 5:17, Paul asks us to "pray without ceasing" (NKJV).

In Romans 15:30–31, the apostle requested prayer from the saints:

> Now I beg you, brethren, through the Lord Jesus Christ, and through the love of the Spirit, that you strive together with me in prayers to God for me. that I may be delivered from those in Judea who do not believe, and that my service for Jerusalem may be acceptable to the saints (NKJV).

In 2 Corinthians 10:4, Paul said, "For the weapons of our warfare are not carnal but mighty in God for pulling down strongholds" (NKJV). In Colossians 2:1, the apostle said, "For I want you to know what a great conflict I have for you and those in Laodicea, and for as many as have not seen my face in the flesh" (NKJV).

Paul talked about his suffering and his fight: "But even after we had suffered before and were spitefully treated at Philippi, as you know, we were bold in our God to speak to you the gospel of God in much conflict" (1 Thessalonians 2:2 NKJV).

Paul said in Philippians 1:29–30, "For to you it has been granted on behalf of Christ, not only to believe in Him but also to suffer for His sake, having the same conflict which you saw in me and now hear is in me" (NKJV).

In Colossians 4:2, we read, "Continue earnestly in prayer, being vigilant in it with thanksgiving" (NKJV).

Paul wrote, "Epaphras, who is one of you, a bondservant of Christ, greets you, always laboring fervently for you in prayers, that you may stand perfect and complete in all the will of God" (Colossians 4:12 NKJV).

Jesus prays a lot also for the success of His discipleship ministry. In Matthew 14:23, we can see Him praying all night. At the end of His ministry, we find Jesus in prayer in Gethsemane (Matthew 26:36–44).

White declares, "If we are not willing to make special sacrifices to save souls that are ready to perish, how can we be counted worthy to enter into the city of God?"[25] She states that "the Lord calls for soldiers who will not fail or be discouraged but who will accept the work with all its disagreeable features. He would have us all take Christ for our pattern."[26]

She adds:

> A greater than Joshua is leading on the armies of Israel. One is in our midst, even the Captain of our salvation, who has said for our encouragement, "Lo, I am with you always, even unto the end of the world." "Be of good cheer; I have overcome the world." He will lead us on to absolute victory. What God promises, He is able at any time to perform. And the work He gives His people to do, He is able to accomplish by them.[27]

A Way to Fulfill Your Highest Purpose in Life

I believe that discipleship is God's way of allowing each believer to fulfill his or her highest purpose in life.

White writes, "I had been deeply impressed by scenes that have recently passed before me in the night season. There seemed to be a great movement, a work of revival, going forward in many places. Our people were moving into line, responding to God's call."[28]

She adds that "life on earth is the beginning of life in heaven; education on earth is an initiation into the principles of heaven; the lifework here is a training for the lifework there. What we now are, in character and holy service, is the sure foreshadowing of what we shall be."[29] She mentions, "The church members must work; they must educate themselves, striving to reach the highest standard set before them. The Lord will help them reach if they cooperate with Him."[30]

Cox and Peck (2018) mention that discipleship promotes the highest purpose of life, as it directly impacts eternity.

A Work with Accountability

Everyone has to report to someone. It is an excellent way to grow. Herrington et al. (2003) remark that people could have accountability for their transformation throughout the journey by joining a group of others who are also committed to the transformational journey.

We find accountability in the Bible. Joshua reported to Moses. The twelve and the seventy reported to Jesus. Hull (2007) affirms:

> The apostles sent Peter and John to check out Philip's budding ministry. Though they wanted to multiply their efforts, the twelve also wanted quality control. They needed evidence that God's hand was in the Samaritans' acceptance of Christ. Surely Peter and John spoke with converts, questioning them concerning their decisions. To be sure God had broken down this barrier, they would pray for the Samaritans to receive the Holy Spirit the way they had received Him. So, they prayed, and the Samaritans received the Spirit, praising God in unknown tongues. God had confirmed the destruction of the Samaritan barrier; the reality of His power could not be denied. Based on this, Peter and John preached on their way home, through Samaritan cities. Their actions reflected a major change in their worldview.[31]

Hull writes:

> Whenever the church multiplies ministry, delegated authority requires accountability. Without it, the multiplied ministry is trouble looking for a place to happen. Pollution of the

message, imitation of methods, misappropriation of gifts, and financial corruption are but a few hazards slackness courts.[32]

He adds:

> Disciples are the product; baptizing and teaching to obey are the qualifiers. At a minimum, a disciple goes public in his witness, through baptism, and submits to the authority of others by being taught. He is available for training; he understands the virtue of accountability. He commits himself to a lifetime of learning. No disciple-making occurs without accountability.[33]

In his classic book on discipleship, Ron Bennett builds upon Moore's definition when he states, "Discipleship is a process that takes place within accountable relationships within a period of time for the purpose of bringing believers to spiritual maturity in Christ."[34] An accountable relationship is significant in understanding the meaning of discipleship. Disciples must be accountable to someone.[35]

Many people need help maintaining their commitments to God. The church should provide a variety of means to hold people accountable. Disciple-making cannot occur if this element is left out. A series of agreements may be made within the discipling program of the church. Both formal and informal means of accountability should be provided—everything from the buddy system to relational covenants.

Hull says:

> All successful ministry is based on relationships. The discipling church should make community building a very high priority, and all church-group life should encourage people to share their needs. A loving and supportive environment builds emotional equity that acts as a cushion during the bumps and turbulence of ministry. This emotional anchor needs to be unleashed to form the church's relational foundation. To keep discipling effective, remember: discipling is not an event; it is a process. No system can make a disciple, because discipleship requires that a person's will be activated by the Holy Spirit.[36]

> No system can make a disciple, because discipleship requires that a person's will be activated by the Holy Spirit.

A Work with Excessive Joy

A disciple of Jesus has joy (John 15:11). White mentions, "It is a mistake to entertain the thought that God is pleased to see His children suffer. All heaven is interested in the happiness of man. Our heavenly Father does not close the avenues of joy to any of His creatures."[37]

She adds:

> Joy—it is the reward of Christ's workers to enter into His joy. That joy, to which Christ Himself looks forward with eager desire, is presented in His request to His Father, "I will say that they also, whom Thou hast given Me, be with Me where I am."[38]

A Rewarding Work

White writes, "The approval of the Master is not given because of the greatness of the work performed, because many things have been gained, but because of the fidelity in even a few things. It is not the great results we attain, but the motives from which we act, that weigh with God. He prizes goodness and faithfulness more than the greatness of the work accomplished."[39]

> Every effort made for Christ will react in blessing upon ourselves.

She adds, "Every effort made for Christ will react in blessing upon ourselves."[40] She writes, "Every duty performed, every sacrifice made in the name of Jesus brings an exceedingly great reward. In the very act of duty, God speaks and gives His blessing."[41]

Harrington (2017) writes that only Jesus is worthy of being the most important thing in our lives—this is discipleship. The principal focus is Jesus, and it is because of who Jesus is and what He said and did that discipleship and disciple-making must be our driving passion.

White writes, "One soul is of infinite value, for Calvary speaks its worth. One soul, won to the truth, will be instrumental in winning others, and there will be an ever-increasing result of blessing and salvation."[42] She adds, "In working for perishing souls, you have the companionship of angels."[43]

Babcock (2002) says there is nothing more thrilling than seeing a person who has come to know Christ become discipled and, in turn, begin to disciple others. He or she has become equipped to reproduce. Reproducers are people who become trainers after they have been trained.

White mentions, "Our little world under the curse of sin—the one dark blot in His glorious creation—will be honored above all other worlds in the universe of God."[44]

She says:

> The humblest and weakest of the disciples of Jesus could be a blessing to others. They may not realize that they are doing any good, but by their unconscious influence, they may start waves of blessing that will widen and deepen; the blessed results they may never know until the day of final reward. They do not feel or know that they are doing anything significant. They are not required to weary themselves with anxiety about success. They have only to go forward quietly, doing faithfully the work that God's providence assigns, and their lives will not be in vain. Their own souls will grow more and more into the likeness of Christ; they are workers together with God in this life and are thus fitting for the higher work and the unshadowed joy of the life to come.[45]

> **The humblest and weakest of the disciples of Jesus could be a blessing to others.**

Making disciples is the mission of every disciple—to go out and seek people for Christ. We are to tell them that God loves them and that there is no time to lose. We are to go to them with love as our tool and bring them to the kingdom of love.

Blessed is that servant whom his master, when he comes, will find so doing (Matthew 24:46 NKJV)

Personal Application

I do not want to be satisfied with my actual spiritual life. I do not want to settle for less when God has more for me. I want to experience the joy of being a disciple.

Suggested Prayers

1. Jesus, give me the joy of being Your disciple.
2. O Lord, help me to grow spiritually.
3. Holy Spirit, fill me as never before so I can fulfill the highest purpose of my life.

CHAPTER 7

CHOSEN TO BE A DISCIPLE OF CHRIST IN THE TWENTY-FIRST CENTURY

"God has not promised to bless our good motives, dreams, and innovation. He has promised to bless His plan; that plan is that disciples make other disciples—everything else is a sideshow."

—Bill Hull

This chapter has a story. I was finished with the previous six chapters and thought that I was done. I sent the chapters to my two sons and asked them to give me their feedback. God inspired my second son, David, to tell me, "Papa, what you wrote is fine, but how can a person be a disciple in this busy world when many work two jobs and others face so many challenges to survive?"

I thought these questions were so right. Let's face this reality.

In every generation, starting with Abraham, God chose people to follow Him. In every generation after His ascension, Jesus selects people to be disciples and to make disciples. The order is to make disciples until the end. Read Matthew 28:18–20 again:

> Jesus came and spoke to them, saying, "All authority has been given to Me in heaven and on earth. Go therefore and make disciples of all the nations, baptizing them in the name of the Father and of the Son and of the Holy Spirit, teaching them to observe all things that I have commanded you; and lo, I am with you always, even to the end of the age" (NKJV).

Amen. It is clear that Jesus will have disciples until the end. It is evident that Jesus also wants disciples in the twenty-first century.

The big question now is: how are we to be disciples in this twenty-first century, when pastors, local church leaders, and members are so busy? How are we to be disciples today in the fourth industrial revolution? How are we to be disciples in this 5G environment, where the fifth-generation wireless technology for digital cellular networks has the potential to change so many things?

Refocus in This Age of Information

We are living in the age of information. We are living in a digital culture. While the internet is a fantastic tool, we must be cautious not to kill our time with God.

Greg McKeown writes, "If you don't prioritize your life, someone else will" and adds that "the disciplined pursuit of less

If you don't prioritize your life, someone else will.

allows us to regain control of our choices so we can make the highest possible contribution towards the things that really matter."[1] In his book, *Essentialism: The Disciplined Pursuit of Less*, McKeown tells the story of Bill Gates, the CEO of Microsoft, who "regularly takes a week off twice a year from his busy and frenetic time to create time and space to seclude himself and do nothing but read articles and books, study technology and think about the big picture."[2] Bill Gates calls these two weeks "Think Week."

Daniel J. Levitin (2015), in his book *The Organized Mind*, writes about the need to be organized in order to manage the deluge of information that assaults us every day. Thomas Kersting (2016), in his book *Disconnected*, gives some alarming statistics about how the overuse of electronic devices can affect the brain.

You must take control of digital gadgets and use them strategically. If not, they will control you and eventually destroy your spiritual life, your personal health, and your family life. In everything, we must cultivate temperance. This is one of the fruits of the Holy Spirit (Galatians 5:23 NKJV). That means if you are addicted to the internet, the Holy Spirit can give you victory over it. If you want to be a disciple of Jesus in this twenty-first century, do not let anything steal your daily time with Jesus. It's during this daily time with Jesus that you will hear His voice; you will find the strength to carry the burden of the day and have a new vision to navigate the challenges of the day. This is where you will find your joy. You will discover the purpose of your life.

Find Time for Yourself and God

Throughout the Bible, we see that nobody can follow God or do something for God without a personal encounter with Him. That is true in this century—to be Jesus's disciple, you must find time to be with Him. Time spent in His presence is never wasted time. It's renewing time, rejuvenating time. Life today is so touching. You cannot navigate all the turns and twists on your own. You need Jesus on your side every day.

You need to seek God every day. He is your Father. He loves you. And in His model prayer in Matthew 6:9–15, Jesus teaches us that God is our Father. He knows our needs. Every day, He will provide for our food. He will give us protection, guidance, and the joy of forgiveness. If there was ever a time when you needed to seek God, it is precisely in these last days. You do not have to navigate this tough life alone. Your Father is waiting for you every day to do for you "exceedingly abundantly above all that we ask or think, according to the power that works in us" (Ephesians 3:20 NKJV).

Make it the priority of your life to spend time with Jesus every day. When you start by spending five or ten minutes with Him every day, after some time, you will begin to devote more because the closer you are to Jesus, the more you'll want to spend time with Him and the more clarity you'll have in your life, and you will experience the joy of walking with Jesus.

Example of Joshua

I do not think that you can have a busier life than Joshua from the Bible. He was someone who had to conquer vast territories occupied by many nations with fortified cities.

According to Joshua 12:7–24, Joshua defeated thirty-one kings on the west side of Jordan, not to mention the kings in the southern and northern areas around the Sea of Galilee. He had to fight enemies all his life. Today, you cannot have more burdens in life than Joshua had. However, God said to Joshua that for him to succeed in that task, he must find time to read and meditate on the Bible every day.

God said, "This Book of the Law shall not depart from your mouth, but you shall meditate in it day and night, that you may observe to do according to all that is written in it. For then you will make your way prosperous, and then you will have good success" (Joshua 1:8 NKJV).

Do you want to succeed in the crazy pace of life in the twenty-first century? Find time to read and meditate on the Bible every day. Do you have many battles to fight? This is the source of the success in your life. God gives the guarantee that if you do that, He "will make your way prosperous" (Joshua 1:8 NKJV). More than that, "God is with you wherever you go" (Joshua 1:9 NKJV). Take time to meditate on Jesus every day and on His sacrifice, the way they treated Him, His love, His passion, His death, and His resurrection. The more you meditate on Jesus, the more you will become like Him and the more strength you will find to face the challenges of life.

Take out time to meditate and pray every day. Like Joshua, you are also in a real fight. The devil is fighting against you every day. Prayer is your spiritual weapon.

Reformer Martin Luther experienced the power of prayer. Here are some quotes from Martin Luther about prayer:

"I have to hurry all day to get time to pray."

"If I fail to spend two hours in prayer each morning, the devil gets the victory through the day. I have so much business I cannot get on without spending three hours daily in prayer."

"If I should neglect prayer but a single day, I should lose a great deal of the fire of faith."[3]

Be mindful that we could be the last disciples of Jesus on this earth.

Jesus said He would be with us until the end. What a joy to know, on this very day, that Jesus is with us—the One who has all authority on heaven and earth. That can be a relief for us, which can help us to manage our anxiety, stress, and fear of tomorrow. Jesus said He would take care of us. The Bible says, "The very hairs of your head are all numbered" (Matthew 10:30 NKJV).

In these challenging days, Jesus said, "Seek first the kingdom of God and His righteousness, and all these things shall be added to you" (Matthew 6:33 NKJV). He will take care of you and your family. To be a disciple of Jesus today, you need to have more faith in Him, knowing He will *never* let you down. Jesus must be the first, the last, and the best in everything you do. As a disciple of Jesus, no matter what the situation is, you have a bright future before you.

That said, in this noisy world, you need to find time for Jesus every day. Time spent with Jesus is not time wasted; it is receiving the necessary fuel to keep you moving ahead with joy and purpose.

Be an Example for Others

You are a disciple of Jesus, and you follow Him by choice and by grace. You learn from Him every day how to live in the kingdom of God. Paul gives a perfect example of how to be a disciple, and these words are timeless. We need them more than ever in this postmodern era. Paul wrote:

> I have been crucified with Christ; it is no longer I who live, but Christ lives in me; and the life which I now live in the flesh I live by faith in the Son of God, who loved me and gave Himself for me (Galatians 2:20 NKJV).

I have to confess that I never grasped the idea of the verse. I always thought that Paul cultivated this idea at the end of his ministry. It was only after some research that I found that Paul wrote the letter to the Galatians around 49 AD, before his attendance at the Jerusalem Council (see also Acts 15:1–30). That means it was not at the end of his life that Paul said, "I have been crucified with Christ." He said that at the very peak of his ministry, full of challenges, persecutions, lapidation, and imprisonments. That means in this challenging time, in your life full of burdens, Christ can still live in you. "Christ living in me" was a new life for Paul. This is the life of a disciple. Always and every day, you must say, "Christ lives in me."

This journey is not only for Paul. It is for every follower of Christ. Paul himself invites us to imitate him. In 1 Corinthians 4:16, he wrote, "Therefore I urge you, imitate me" (NKJV). In 1 Corinthians 11:1, he says, "Imitate me, just as I also imitate Christ" (NKJV). To Timothy, he declared, "Let no one despise your youth, but be an example to the believers in word, in conduct, in love, in spirit, in faith, in purity" (1 Timothy 4:12 NKJV). To Titus, he wrote, "In all things showing yourself to be a pattern of good works; in doctrine showing integrity, reverence, incorruptibility, sound speech that cannot be condemned, that one who is an opponent may be ashamed, having nothing evil to say of you" (Titus 2:7–8 NKJV). Paul wants the Christian, the disciple, to be a model to others wherever he or she is, learning from Jesus every day.

The disciple learns from Jesus how to do everything he or she does in the manner in which Jesus did it. In this journey, Jesus understands our shortcomings, our weaknesses. He will always keep you going. If Jesus lives in you, and you are Jesus's apprentice, then no matter what your age, race, profession, or social status, you should continuously ask yourself how Jesus would deal with the specific situation.

For example, I am a father of three. I have to ask myself always how Jesus would interact with my children if He was in my place. I encourage you to cultivate this perspective in whatever you are doing in your family, work, church, and the spectrum of your life. That will be possible only by grace and through love. As disciples, we must let Jesus implant His love in us. This love is not natural; only the Holy Spirit can give it to you.

As a disciple, your relationship with Jesus covers everything, religious or secular. Through you, more people will get an idea of who Jesus is.

Paul wrote, "Clearly you are an epistle of Christ, ministered by us, written not with ink but by the Spirit of the living God, not on tablets of stone but on tablets of flesh, that is, of the heart" (2 Corinthians 3:3 NKJV). I hope you will never forget that. *You*—yes, you! —are a letter from Christ to others.

You are not an accident on this earth. You have a specific mission here. From the past eternity, God had the dream for you to follow Jesus, to become like Jesus, to make other disciples for Him. He will do just that for you if you give Him permission. Put your hands in His Hands. Trust Him. This is God's way for you to achieve your destiny in this life. God wants you to experience a life full of joy and fulfillment. You were born for this! This is your highest purpose in this life. You have been *chosen to be a disciple.*

Personal Application

1. "How will I find enough time to spend time with God daily? I'm so busy. I have to work two jobs." Remember that it's because you have a lot to do that you need God the most. If you do not spend quality time with God daily, that's where you will lose the battle.

2. I have to make up my mind that I am a "letter from Christ" to my family, my coworkers, and others.

3. I want to make the resolution today, by God's grace, to find time every day to read and meditate on the Bible. If I do so, I believe the same God who fought for Joshua will also fight for me. He will give me success in my life. I reclaim His promise for success over my life. (Read again Joshua 1:8–9).

4. It's time to burn bridges; there is no coming back to my old spiritual life. By God's grace, I want to be one of the faithful disciples of Jesus in this twenty-first century.

Suggested Prayers

1. O Jesus, I ask You today to give me the willingness and determination to find time every day to read and meditate on the Bible.

2. My Savior and my Lord, I ask You to fight my battles for me as You fought for Joshua in the past.

3. My God helps me to conquer all the territories He has in mind for my family and me.

4. Jesus, despite the busyness of this life, give me the desire and the will through the Holy Spirit to spend time with You in prayer every day.

5. Jesus, help me to live on this earth as Your disciple.

THANK YOU

Thank you so much for purchasing my book.

You could have picked other books, but you chose this one.

So, THANK YOU for getting this book and for making it all the way to the end.

Before you go, I wanted to ask you for one small favor. Could you please consider posting a review on Amazon? Posting a review is the best and easiest way to spread the information of this book.

Your feedback will help me to write the kind of books that will help you in your spiritual growth. It would mean a lot to me to hear from you. Click on this link to leave your review:

https://www.amazon.com/review/create-review?&asin=B0924Y4HZG

APPENDIX A

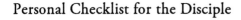

Personal Checklist for the Disciple

1. I read my Bible every day.

2. I spend some personal time with Jesus every day.

3. Every day I worship my Lord.

4. My weekly worship is enhancing.

5. I take time to fast every week or every month, or from time to time.

6. Every year, the Holy Spirit helps me to bring at least one person to Christ.

7. I experience the joy of salvation.

8. I am faithful in my tithes and offerings.

9. I am helping at least one individual at a time to become a disciple of Jesus.

10. I help my church to accomplish the Great Commission.

11. I help my community, even by small acts of kindness.

APPENDIX B

Discipleship Curriculum
Establish a Cyclical System

A. Structural Model 1

B. Structural Model 2

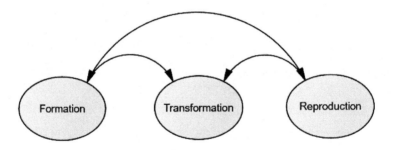

The three steps of this process are formation, transformation, and reproduction.

We have been doing church the same way for years, and we see the results. We are making new converts, not disciples. We are making consumers, not producers. As a result, new believers leave the church every year. We are wasting many lives. Why can we not follow the Great

Commission by making disciples? That will help the church to grow exponentially. It will save many lives.

To apply the discipleship process, the pastor or the church leader must be a believer in discipleship, as Jesus commands and practices.

1. The pastor must train the local church leaders on discipleship (using the chapters of this book).
2. The pastor should train some local church leaders on how to lead a discipleship class.
3. The pastor should preach about discipleship.
4. The pastor should develop, with passion, love for discipleship among church members.

The pastor can try the following steps:

1. A four-month program
2. A one-year discipleship Sabbath school class
3. One-on-one discipling
4. Specialized programs at the church on discipleship
5. Evaluating and repeating the process

DISCIPLE TRAINING

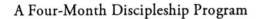

A Four-Month Discipleship Program

A. Know Jesus Better (first month)

1. The life and teaching of Jesus

2. His death

3. The prayer of Jesus

4. How to be a disciple of Jesus

B. Know the Bible Better (second month)

1. The importance and inerrancy of the Bible

2. The prophecy in the Bible

3. The importance of daily Bible reading (Joshua 1, Psalm 1, Psalm 119)

4. Read and apply the Bible as a disciple daily (Joshua 1, Psalm 1, and Psalm 119—those who practice the Word as a rock)

C. Know the Holy Spirit Better (third month)

1. The Holy Spirit in the Bible

2. The Person of the Holy Spirit

3. The work of the Holy Spirit

4. How to be filled with the Holy Spirit as a disciple

D. Know the Discipleship Procedure Better (fourth month)

1. The Great Commission

2. The mission of each believer

3. How to make other disciples I (John 15—interior fruit, character)

4. How to make other disciples II (John 15—exterior fruit, make other disciples)

A One-Year Discipleship Program
(Through a Sabbath School class or other small groups)

Have a special discipleship class each Sabbath morning for new converts for a year. Go over the lesson for ten minutes and start with a unique course on discipleship. This class must have at least two teachers.

Start with the four-month program on discipleship. After that, cover the following topics:

1. The importance of prayer
2. The importance of reading the Bible daily
3. Seek the baptism of the Holy Spirit
4. Every new believer must become a disciple of Jesus (follow Him, self-deny, carry his/her cross)
5. Practice the spiritual disciplines (prayer, fasting, worship at home and in the church, witness, etc.)
6. Fasting in the life of the disciple
7. Weekly worship (come with a friend or a family member)
8. The importance and power of intercessory prayer
9. How to hold a Bible study in person, via Zoom or over the phone
10. How to be prepared for the evangelistic campaign
11. How to work in an evangelistic campaign

12. What to do after an evangelistic campaign (contact with and care for new converts)

13. How to become a disciple of Jesus

14. How to lead a Bible study

15. How to lead a person to Christ

16. How to make new disciples for Jesus

17. Justification

18. Sanctification

19. The twenty-eight fundamental doctrines (one doctrine per week)

20. Ellen G. White and her writings (read three books for the year: *Steps to Christ*, *The Desire of Ages*, and *The Great Controversy*)

- One-on-one discipleship
- Specialized programs at the church on discipleship
- Evaluate and repeat the process

Throughout the training, you and the local church leaders will pray, asking the Lord and His Holy Spirit for the three steps of the process: formation, transformation, and reproduction.

ACKNOWLEDGMENTS

I praise the Lord for putting this burden on my heart to write on discipleship. His grace helped me throughout the process of writing and publishing this book. I can say, "All my springs are in you" (Psalm 87:7 NKJV).

A book is never a solitary endeavor. So many people have given me significant support to finish this work. I may forget some, but I would like to especially thank the following people:

- My loving wife, Gina, and three children, Ginaldy, David, and Daniela, for their support and encouragement. They always encourage me to do more. I never could have finished this book without the sacrificial help of Gina and some amazing insights from my children. My family is my true inspiration. I will be forever grateful for their unconditional love.

- Lourise, Annalee Simone, and Evelynn Marie for their special encouragement.

- Camille Lauren for her expertise.

- The church members, the members of Parole Delivrance Ministries, and the professors and students of the PhD Cohort 2017 for their support.

- Gerson P. Santos, Tony Anobile, Jose Cortes Jr., G. Earl Knight, Pierre Omeler, Jose Joseph, Bordes Henry Saturne, Daniel Honore, Henry Beras, Alanzon Smith, Reginald Barthelemy,

Ainsworth E. Joseph, Pedro Conzales, Stephen Wayne Pilgrim, Juan Carlos Niño de Guzmán Miranda, Jose Girarte, Manuel Rosario, Ariel Manzuete, Samuel Peguero, Smith Olivier, Geodaly Augustin, Price and Sylvie Reveil, Yves Pierre, Came and Joseph Charles for their support.

- The ethnics ministries coordinators and directors of the Greater New York Conference
- The pastors and laypeople from all ethnic groups at the Greater New York Conference and the Northeastern Conference.

ENDORSEMENTS FOR THE BOOK

———————◄◆—◆—◆►———————

During the last few decades, Seventh-day Adventist membership records reported a loss of about forty percent. It is worthwhile to remember that membership loss is not unique to this denomination. In recent years, North American mainline denominations lost one-third of their membership. Christian leaders attribute the current situation to faulty discipleship. The foundational problem of the church is that it embodies superficial discipleship. Dr. Charles reminds us of some essential biblical considerations on discipleship, answering some of the most important questions regarding this important topic.

Gerson P. Santos, DMin
Associate Secretary, General Conference of Seventh-day Adventists

***

In a time when a majority of church members seem to be content with their church attendance, and others appear to think that participation in nurturing seminars within the safe and comfortable physical (or virtual) walls of the church makes them disciples, Jesus is looking for followers. Followers who have received His grace, people who share the priorities of their master, disciples who love, seek, and partner with Him to save relatives, neighbors, and co-workers. Disciples who will not be satisfied till they lead someone to the feet of their Savior.

In this book, Dr. Robert J. Charles shares his heart as a disciple. His clear Biblical understanding of the calling plus the very practical applications to a life of discipleship make this book a must-read.

Jose Cortes Jr., Associate Ministerial Director for Evangelism
North American Division of Seventh-day Adventists

***

In his book Chosen as a Disciple, Dr. R. Jean-Marie Charles has done an excellent job in explaining the importance and process of discipleship. He has pointed out that as a church, we are losing approximately forty percent of the members we have added since 1965. This is a serious problem that Dr Charles has made several recommendations of how we can close the "back door" of the church. May the reading of this book serve to give us a better understanding of discipleship.

G. Earl Knight
President, Atlantic Union Conference

***

Chosen to Be a Disciple is a passionate cry from the heart of a spiritual leader who can attest to the dire need for authentic discipleship in our churches. Denouncing the machination of the devil who resorts to obfuscation to stagnate the ascendant journey of God's people, Dr. Charles offers clear and practical guidelines for a coherent and meaningful approach to spiritual growth. This timely publication will help God's chosen people to thrive in an antagonistic world and attain "the whole measure of the fullness of Christ" (Ephesians 4:13 NIV).

Pastor Bordes Henry Saturné, MEd, MTh, PhD
Chair, Andrews University Leadership Department

***

This book has been inspired by God. It comes exactly at the right time where the World Church leadership is focusing on the same goal "Make disciple". The strategies using in the book of Dr. Jean-Marie Robert Charles make the evangelism work easy and practical to everyone desiring to use Christ's method to prepare for His soon coming. As we are approaching the last days, our God is enlightening the best way to fulfill our mission by leaving our comfort zone to reach more souls for his kingdom. Yes, this book: "Chosen to be a disciple" comes on time. I highly recommend it to all Christian believers. In reading this book, let's pray that the Holy Spirit leads us in action as he did for the Christians of the early Church so that we can be participants in the last great evangelism explosion of the world.

Jose L Joseph, ND. CFLE. Vice-President
Atlantic Union Conference
Franco-Haitian Caucus Director
North American Division

***

I admire the courage and character of the author to address a most relevant, practical, and necessary issue, that of discipleship. The wisdom of bringing to the discussion the correlation between the concept of membership versus the concept of discipleship is splendid. In other words, the injunction given by Christ was not to make members but to make disciples, because disciples do not become stagnant or plateau, but grow.

Therefore, to do otherwise would be to lose the integrity of our mission and the calling of Christ.

The beauty of the book, however, is to be found in its practicality. It answers the questions "Why be a disciple?", "How to be a disciple?" and "What does a disciple do?" In the "why", "how", and "what" lie the answers to the fulfillment of being chosen to be a disciple. It helps the reader understand and explore the necessity of being a disciple of Christ, especially in the 21st century. I strongly recommend this book to all pastors, leaders, officers and members. It is not a replication of the other books on discipleship, but a fresh look at a pertinent subject with clarity and honesty. Most of all, the conclusions drawn and the implications given are based on Biblical principles.

Dr. Alanzo Smith
Executive Secretary, Greater New York Conference

***

I would highly recommend this book to all readers who want to deepen their knowledge about discipleship. In this book, in addition to exploring the critical issues of discipleship, Dr. Charles skillfully investigates the substance of discipleship. Whether you are interested in knowing how to be a good disciple or you want to know how to make other disciples, this book is a must-read for you. *Chosen to Be a Disciple* should be in the library of anyone who desires to excel in the mission of making disciples.

Dr. Pierre E. Omeler
Executive Secretary, Atlantic Union Conference

***

For many years the Church has followed a distorted concept of the Great Commission which places emphasis on obtaining the highest number of baptisms. The unintended consequence has resulted in the increased spiritual mortality of the church. Membership rolls fill up while the pews empty out. Robert J. Charles passionately challenges us to re-envision the Great Commission through the lens of discipleship. At its core, discipleship is not about adding numbers to the roster but rather about reconciling sinners with a loving God. The command to make disciples compels us to empower others by teaching them the path to an everlasting relationship with God. The author's simple, yet profound, approach to soulwinning recalibrates our approach to evangelism by prompting us to refocus on the need for long-term commitment to Christ and His Cause.

Daniel Honore
President, Northeastern Conference of Seventh-day Adventists

***

Chosen to Be a Disciple is a must-read book for all those who desire to become disciples of Christ and make disciples for Christ. It is not just theoretical, but very practical. Robert J. Charles has done an exceptional job of reminding us that the key to spiritual growth is in spending time with God and the reading of the Bible. He teaches us steps to become disciples and to reach more people for the kingdom of God. This book is definitely valuable for pastors, leaders, lay members, and families all around the world. I believe all those who read this book will be blessed by it. It will certainly lead people to a closer walk with Jesus. I highly recommend this book to everyone who longs for that type of relationship.

Reginald R. Barthelemy, DMin, PhD
Ministerial Secretary & Men's Ministries Director,
Greater New York Conference of Seventh-day Adventists

***

The book *Chosen to Be a Disciple* reflects a God-given passion of Robert J. Charles, stirring a vision that addresses a growing phenomenon in the Seventh-day Adventist Church and, I dare say, Christian denominations in general. There are some things about this book that make it a must-read. **Firstly,** it avoids complex use of language, which renders it reader-friendly. **Secondly,** it helps the reader to understand their personal role and relationship to Christ and the Church as a disciple of Jesus. Each chapter ends with a personal application and a recommended prayer. **Thirdly,** it offers practical steps to becoming an effective disciple. **Fourthly,** it is grounded on scripture, which separates it from other works that may be mere human ideas on the subject. **Finally,** it was developed through an empirical study and design. Therefore, the academic mind can also be engaged and conversant with the contents.

Chosen to Be a Disciple will prove to be insightful and relevant to the times. The contents are transcultural. Hence, pastors can use it as an additional resource for discipleship training with their congregation. Thus, it is with great delight that I endorse and recommend *Chosen to Be a Disciple* as a timely and useful publication.

Ainsworth E. Joseph, PhD, DMin
Ministerial Director, Northeastern Conference

***

Dr. Charles has undoubtedly hit the mark, and it was not revealed by blood or flesh. I love how he connects discipleship with crucial aspects such as the Holy Spirit's work, the ministry of Jesus, and the church's multiplication process. Also, the book's structure of why, how, and what is brilliant and didactic. I congratulate the author and encourage you to read, apply, and share it. Let us receive this bread from heaven with gratitude and thanksgiving.

Dr. Manuel A. Rosario
Personal Ministries and Sabbath School Director,
Greater New York Conference of Seventh-day Adventists

***

I was inspired and motivated as I read *Chosen to Be a Disciple*. Dr. Charles has produced a well documented and practical book for discipleship. He writes with passion and sincerity, drawing from the inspired writings and a long line of researchers and authors passionate about the subject. Here the reader will find practical ideas that will encourage them in their discipleship journey, and church leaders will find tools to develop a discipleship strategy for their congregations. I wish every youth and young adult would take the time to feast on these pages.

Pr. Lt. Ariel Manzueta
Youth Director, Greater New York Conference

***

I believe that every church member should read this book. We welcome this new publication by Dr. Robert J. Charles. *Chosen to Be a Disciple* is a spiritual, practical and well-documented resource that defines and explains the path to successful strategic discipleship. I certainly believe each church member should read this book and put into practice its teachings.

Dr. Samuel Peguero
Family Ministries/Single's Ministries Director
Senior Pastor, Spanish Prospect SDA Church
Greater New York Conference of SDA

AUTHOR BIO

———◆—◆—◆———

Robert J. Charles, PhD, DMin has been involved in ministry for over 30 years, helping adults, young people, and children transform their lives by God's grace. He was an Administrator of the SDA Church, Dean of the Theological Seminary. Currently, he is an Ethnic Ministries Coordinator at the Greater New York Conference SDA Church and Advisor at Andrews University for the Doctor of Ministry Program. His passion is saving souls for Jesus and training others for God's glory. He and his loving wife, Gina, work as a team and have three growing children, Ginaldy, David and Daniela.

ABOUT THE BOOK

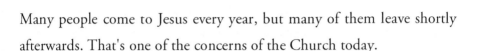

Many people come to Jesus every year, but many of them leave shortly afterwards. That's one of the concerns of the Church today.

Why does this happen? What are the reasons? This book outlines how the non-discipleship culture of Christianity today is one of the main reasons for this problem.

In this book, you will understand the answers to the following questions: Why should you be a disciple? How can you be a disciple? What does a disciple do?

CHOSEN TO BE A DISCIPLE will help YOU to:

1. Know that you are chosen by God for an amazing purpose on this earth

2. Discover the joy and fulfillment of being a disciple

3. Release your full potential as a disciple

4. Live as Christ's disciple in these post-COVID-19 times

5. Enjoy what God has in store for you as a disciple

***

CONTACT THE AUTHOR

To get updates and resources,
visit the website www.robertjcharles.com

REFERENCES

Astley, J. (2015). Forming disciples: Some educational and biblical reflections. *Rural Theology, 13*(1), 4–17. doi:10.1179/1470499415Z.00000000037

Babcock, E. (2002). *The implementation of a disciple-making process in the local church* (Unpublished doctoral thesis). George Fox University. Retrieved from http://digitalcommons.georgefox.edu/dmin/180.

Beard, C. (2015). Missional discipleship: Discerning spiritual-formation practices and goals within the missional movement. *Missiology, 43*(2), 175–194. doi:10.1177/0091829614563059

Begg, A. (2021). Five truths about the Holy Spirit. *Ligonier Ministries.* Retrieved from https://www.ligonier.org/blog/five-truths-about-holy-spirit/.

Bennett, R. (2001). *Intentional disciplemaking: Cultivating spiritual maturity in the local church.* Colorado Springs, CO: NavPress.

Bevans, S. (2018). Transforming discipleship and the future of mission. *International Review of Mission, 107*(2), 362–377. doi:10.1111/irom.12236

rosius, K. M. (2017). Culture and the church's discipleship strategy. *Journal of Ministry & Theology, 21*(1), 123–157. Retrieved from EBSCO database.

Brown, M. R. (2012). *By this they will know: Discipleship principles to transform the church* (Unpublished doctoral thesis). Liberty University. Retrieved from https://digitalcommons.liberty.edu/doctoral/596/.

Bullón, A. (2017). *Total member involvement: A call to serve.* Silver Spring, MD: Review & Herald Publishing Association.

Burggraff, A. (2015). Developing discipleship curriculum: Applying the systems APPROACH model for designing instruction by Dick, Carey, and Carey to the construction of Church discipleship courses. *Christian Education Journal: Research on Educational Ministry, 12*(2), 397–414. doi:10.1177/073989131501200211

Chenou, J. (2014). From cyber-libertarianism to neoliberalism: Internet exceptionalism, multi-stakeholderism, and the institutionalisation of internet governance in the 1990s. *Globalizations, 11*(2), 205–223. doi:10.1080/14747731.2014.887387

Chisholm, D. (2016). *Formulating a covenant of discipleship for the membership of the Gwinnett Church of Christ* (Unpublished doctoral thesis). Abilene Christian University. Retrieved from https://digitalcommons.acu.edu/dmin_theses/25/.

Cho, M. (1990). *Christ-centered discipleship: A biblical concept of religious education* (Unpublished doctoral thesis). Andrews University. Retrieved from https://digitalcommons.andrews.edu/dissertations/279.

Cole, D. E. (2018). *Re-focus: Creating an outward-focused church culture.* Outward-Focused Network.

Cox, W. F. Jr. & Peck, R. A. (2018). Christian education as discipleship formation. *Christian Education Journal, 15*(2), 243–261. doi:10.1177/0739891318778859

Dawson, T. & Dawson, R. (2010). *Refocus: Cutting-edge strategies to evolve your video business*. Berkeley, CA: Peachpit.

Eims, L., & Coleman, R. E. (2009). *The lost art of disciple-making*. Grand Rapids, MI: Zondervan.

Elliott-Hart, T. M. (2011). *Educating for discipleship in consumer culture: Promising practices rooted in the pastoral circle* (Unpublished doctoral dissertation). Boston College. Retrieved from http://hdl.handle.net/2345/1942.

Francis, J. M. M. (2015). Learning church: Theology for discipleship and ministry. *Rural Theology, 13*(1), 97–101. doi:10.1179/1470499415Z.00000000045

Francis, L. J., Foster, S., Lankshear, D. W., & Jones, I. (2019). What helps Christians grow? An exploratory study distinguishing among four distinctive pathways. *Pastoral Psychology, 68*(4), 379–392. doi:10.1007/s11089-019-00866-5

Frederick, T. V. (2008). Discipleship and spirituality from a Christian perspective. *Pastoral Psychology, 56*(6), 553–560. doi:10.1007/s11089-008-0148-8

Gallo, C. (2019). The art of persuasion hasn't changed in 2,000 years. *Harvard Business Review*. Retrieved from https://hbr.org/2019/07/the-art-of-persuasion-hasnt-changed-in-2000-

years?utm_medium=email&utm_source=newsletter_daily&utm_ca mpaign=mtod_notactsubs.

Ghazaryan Drissi, A. (2019). What is transforming discipleship? *The Ecumenical Review, 71*(1–2), 216–224. doi:10.1111/erev.12421

Green IV, J. T. (2012). *An analysis of the discipleship strategy of Robert Emerson Coleman* (Unpublished doctoral dissertation). The Southern Baptist Theological Seminary. Retrieved from https://digital.library.sbts.edu/handle/10392/3963?show=full.

Gushiken, K. M. (2015). Cultivating healthy discipleship settings in multi-ethnic churches. *Transformation: An International Journal of Holistic Mission Studies, 32*(1), 17–26. doi:10.1177/0265378814537753

Haigh, T., Russell, A. L., & Dutton, W. H. (2015). *Histories of the Internet: Introducing a Special Issue of Information & Culture, 50*(2), 143–159. doi:10.7560/IC50201

Harrington, B., & Putman, J. (2013). *DiscipleShift: Five steps that help your church to make disciples who make disciples.* Grand Rapids, MI: Zondervan.

Hawkins, A., Kinnaman, D., & Matlock, M. (2019). *Faith for exiles: 5 ways for a new generation to follow Jesus in Digital Babylon.* Grand Rapids, MI: Baker Books.

Hewitt, R. R. (2014). Evangelism as discipleship: Implications for theological education and leadership formation. *International Review of Mission, 103*(399), 200–214. doi:10.1111/irom.12057

Hilgemann, B. (2018). 12 spiritual disciplines that will make your faith strong. *Church Leaders.* Retrieved from https://churchleaders.com/outreach-missions/outreach-missions-articles/325192-12-spiritual-disciplines-that-will-make-your-faith-strong-brandon-hilgemann.html.

Hull, B. (2006). *The complete book of discipleship: On being and making followers of Christ.* Colorado Springs, CO: NavPress.

Hull, B. (2007). *Disciple-making pastor—Leading others on the journey of faith.* Ada, MI: Baker Publishing Group.

Hull, B. (2010). *The disciple-making church: Leading a body of believers on the journey of faith.* Grand Rapids, MI: Baker Books.

Jahnel, C. (2018). Discipleship in creative (un)certainty. *International Review of Mission, 107*(2), 428–442. doi:10.1111/irom.12241

Jordan, E. (2015). All God's people facing the same way: A theology of discipleship shaped by disciples—an Anglican perspective. *Journal of Adult Theological Education, 12*(2), 153–158. doi:10.1179/1740714115Z.00000000043

Kaplan, R. S., & Norton, D. P. (2006). *Alignment: Using the balanced scorecard to create corporate synergies.* Boston: Harvard Business Review Press.

Kidder, S. J. (2015). *Moving your church: Becoming a spirit-led community.* Nampa, ID: Pacific Press Publishing Association.

Knight, G. E. (2019). Closing the back door. *Atlantic Union Gleaner, 118*(11), 3. Retrieved from https://atlanticuniongleaner.org/editorials/2019/closing-the-back-door/.

Kotiuga, N. (2017). *Spiritual formation in the workplace* (Unpublished doctoral thesis). Bakke Graduate University. Retrieved from https://www.bgu.edu/dissertations/spiritual-formation-workplace-discipleship-happens-work/

Lang, J. A., & Bochman, J. (2017). Positive outcomes of a discipleship process. *Journal of Spiritual Formation & Soul Care, 10*(1), 51–72.

Lynn, J. (2014). *Making disciples of Jesus Christ: Investigating, identifying, and implementing an effective discipleship system* (Unpublished doctoral dissertation). Liberty University. Retrieved from https://digitalcommons.liberty.edu/doctoral/878.

Martin Luther Prayer Quotations. (2019). Retrieved from https://www.quotetab.com/martin-luther-quotes-about-prayer.

McKnight, S. (2016). *The King Jesus Gospel: The original good news revisited*. Grand Rapids, MI: Zondervan.

Meyers, R. A. (2010). Unleashing the power of worship. *Anglican Theological Review, 92*(1), 55–70. Retrieved from http://www.anglicantheologicalreview.org/wp-content/uploads/2020/03/meyers_92.1.pdf.

Moore, W. B. (2013). *The multiplier: Making disciple makers*. New York: Christ Disciples Ministries.

Murrell, S., & Murrell, W. (2016). *The multiplication challenge: A strategy to solve your leadership shortage*. Lake Mary, FL.: Creation House, Charisma House.

Onyinah, O. (2017). The meaning of discipleship. *International Review of Mission, 106*(2), 216–227. doi:10.1111/irom.12181

Peterson, D. (2002). *Engaging with God: A biblical theology of worship*. Downers Grove, IL: InterVarsity Press.

Roxburgh, A. J., & Romanuk, F. (2020). *The missional leader: Equipping your church to reach a changing world*. Minneapolis, MN: Fortress Press.

Seifert, V. M. (2013). *Discipleship as a catalyst for personal transformation in the Christian faith* (Unpublished doctoral dissertation). University of the Incarnate Word. Retrieved from https://athenaeum.uiw.edu/uiw_etds/45.

Shirley, C. (2016). Discipleship it takes a church to make a disciple: An integrative model of discipleship for the Church. *Southwestern Journal of Theology, 50*(2). Retrieved from https://www.semanticscholar.org/paper/Discipleship-it-takes-a-church-to-make-a-disciple-%3A-Shirley/891cef04e875db940b422c93ad36a5d81fa8a094.

Smith, D. (2014). *A pastor's approach to discipleship and its effect on the local church: A three-step approach to biblical discipleship* (Unpublished doctoral dissertation). Liberty University. Retrieved from https://digitalcommons.liberty.edu/doctoral/842.

Takala, T. (1997). Charismatic leadership: A key factor in organizational communication. *Corporate Communications: An International Journal, 2*(1), 8–13. doi:10.1108/eb046529

Tangenberg, K. (2012). Congregational mentoring and discipleship: Implications for social work practice. *Journal of Religion & Spirituality in Social Work: Social Thought, 31*(3), 285–302. doi:10.1080/15426432.2012.679844

Thomas, H., ed. (2015). *Mentor's guide: A companion resource to the Discipleship Handbook.* Michigan: The Training Center Church Committee of the Michigan Conference of Seventh-day Adventists.

Travis, J. (1965). Discipline in the new testament. *Pastoral Psychology, 16*(9), 12–21. doi:10.1007/bf01793446

Trim, D. (2018). Statistical report: Missions trends and progress. *Adventist Archives.* Retrieved from https://www.adventistresearch.org/node/334.

Tyrrell, J. (2019). Jesus cares: We must care too! *Atlantic Union Gleaner, 118*(11), 5–7.

Walton, R. (2011). Disciples together: The small group as a vehicle for discipleship formation. *Journal of Adult Theological Education, 8*(2), 99–114. doi:10.1558/JATE.v8i2.99

Wester, R., & Koster, J. (2015). The software behind Moore's Law. *Computer, 46*(10), 66–72. doi:10.1109/MC.2013.7

Wheeler, A. (2015). The commissioning of all believers: Toward a more holistic model of global discipleship. *Missiology, 43*(2), 148–162. doi:10.1177/0091829614541093

White, E. G. (2002). *Christian service: A compilation.* Hagerstown, MD: Review and Herald Pub. Association.

———. *A Solemn Appeal* [Kindle Cloud Reader version].

———. *Testimonies for the Church*, vol. 2 [Kindle Cloud Reader version].

———. *Testimonies for the Church*, vol. 4 [Kindle Cloud Reader version].

———. *Testimonies for the Church*, vol. 5 [Kindle Cloud Reader version].

———. *Testimonies for the Church*, vol. 6 [Kindle Cloud Reader version].

———. *Testimonies for the Church*, vol. 8 [Kindle Cloud Reader version].

———. Testimonies for the Church, vol. 9 [Kindle Cloud Reader version].

———. *Counsels to Parents, Teachers, and Students*, location 6073 20 [Kindle Cloud Reader version].

———. *The Great Controversy* [Kindle Cloud Reader version].

———. *Christian Service* [Kindle Cloud Reader version].

———. *The Desire of Ages* [Kindle Cloud Reader version].

———. *Pastoral Ministry* [Kindle Cloud Reader version].

———. *The Acts of the Apostles* [Kindle Cloud Reader version].

———. *Evangelism* [Kindle Cloud Reader version].

———. *Christian Integrity in the Ministry* [Kindle Cloud Reader version].

———. *The Youth's Instructor* [Kindle Cloud Reader version].

———. *Spiritual Disciplines for the Christian Life* [Kindle Cloud Reader version].

———. *Christ's Object Lessons* [Kindle Cloud Reader version].

———. *Gospel Workers* [Kindle Cloud Reader version].

———. *Prophets and Kings* [Kindle Cloud Reader version].

———. *Education* [Kindle Cloud Reader version].

———. *Steps to Christ* [Kindle Cloud Reader version].

Whitmore, W. (2018). The branch is linked to the vine. *International Review of Mission, 107*(2), 472–482. doi:10.1111/irom.12244

Whitney, D. S. (2014). *Spiritual disciplines for the Christian life (revised and updated).* Colorado Springs, CO: NavPress.

Willard, D. (2006). *The great omission: Reclaiming Jesus's essential teachings on discipleship.* San Francisco: HarperOne.

Wilson, T., Ferguson, D., Hirsch, A., & Stetzer, E. (2019). *Becoming a level five multiplying church: Field guide.* Carolina Beach, NC: Exponential.

NOTES

CHAPTER 1

[1] David Trim (2018). "Statistical Report: Missions Trends and Progress." *Adventist Archives.*

[2] "Ellen G. White (1827-1915) is considered the most widely translated American author, her works having been published in more than 160 languages. She wrote more than 100,000 pages on a wide variety of spiritual practical topics. Guided by the Holy Spirit, she exalted Jesus and pointed to the Scriptures as the basis of one's faith" (UNASP, "Life Sketches of James White and Ellen G. White 1888"). Smithsonian Magazine has named her one of the 100 Most Significant Americans of All Time.

[3] Ellen G. White (1898). *Desire of Ages.* Mountain View: Pacific Press Publishing Association, p. 116.

[4] Joi Tyrrell (2019). "Jesus Cares: We Must Care Too!" *Atlantic Union Gleaner, 118*(11), 5–7.

[5] Bill Hull (2007). *The Disciple-Making Pastor*, p. 21 [Kindle Cloud Reader version].

[6] G. Earl Knight (2019). "Closing the Back Door," *Atlantic Union Gleaner, 118*(11), 3.

[7] Scot McKnight (2011). *The King Jesus: The Original Good News Revisited.* Grand Rapids, MI: Zondervan, p. 18.

[8] Ellen G. White (2010). *Testimonies for the Church*, vol. 8, p. 215 [Kindle Cloud Reader version].

[9] Bill Hull (2007). *Disciple-Making Pastor: Leading Others on the Journey of Faith.* Grand Rapids: Baker Publishing Group, p. 70.

[10] White, *Testimonies for the Church*, vol. 4, p. 155 [Kindle Cloud Reader version].

[11] Ellen G. White (2010). *Counsels to Parents, Teachers, and Students,* location 6073 20 [Kindle Cloud Reader version].

[12] Ellen G. White (2010). *Christian Service*, p. 32 [Kindle Cloud Reader version].

[13] White, *Testimonies for the Church*, vol. 6, p. 426. [Kindle Cloud Reader version].

[14] White, *Christian Service*, p. 30.

[15] White, *Pastoral Ministry*, p. 157 [Kindle Cloud Reader version].

[16] White, *Christian Service,* p. 101.

[17] White, *The Desire of Ages*, p. 135 [Kindle Cloud Reader version].

[18] White, *The Desire of Ages*, p. 54.

CHAPTER 2

[1] Hull, *The Complete Book of Discipleship*, p. 60 [Kindle Cloud Reader version].

[2] Tirrell M. Elliott-Hart (2011). Educating for Discipleship in Consumer Culture: Promising Practices Rooted in the Pastoral Circle, p. 42.

[3] White, The Desire of Ages, p. 6 [Kindle Cloud Reader version].

[4] White, *The Desire of Ages,* p. 250 [Kindle Cloud Reader version].

[5] White, *The Acts of the Apostles*, p. 45.

[6] White, *The Desire of Ages*, p. 4 [Kindle Cloud Reader version].

[7] Ellen G. White (1906). *Review and Herald*, p. 21.

[8] Ellen G. White (1891). *Letter 50*–1891, p. 4.

[9] White, *The Acts of the Apostles*, p. 57 [Kindle Cloud Reader version].

[10] Ellen G. White, *Evangelism*, p. 459 [Kindle Cloud Reader version].

[11] White, *Christian Service*, p. 166 [Kindle Cloud Reader version].

[12] White, *The Desire of Ages*, p. 130 [Kindle Cloud Reader version].

[13] Mark R. Brown (2012). *By This They Will Know: Discipleship Principles to Transform the Church*, p. 70.

[14] Ellen G. White (1886). *Christian Integrity in the Ministry*, pp. 5–6.

[15] White, *Christian Integrity in the Ministry*, pp. 8–11.

[16] White, The Desire of Ages, p. 13 [Kindle Cloud Reader version].

[17] White, *The Acts of the Apostles*, pp. 163–164 [Kindle Cloud Reader version].

[18] White, *The Desire of Ages*, p. 362 [Kindle Cloud Reader version].

[19] White, *The Desire of Ages*, p. 136 [Kindle Cloud Reader version].

[20] Alistair Begg (2021). *Five Truths About the Holy Spirit*. Ligonier Ministries.

21 White, *The Desire of Ages*, p. 131 [Kindle Cloud Reader version].

22 Donald S. Whitney (2014). *Spiritual Disciplines for the Christian Life*, p. 291 [Kindle Cloud Reader version].

23 White, *Christian Service,* p. 180.

24 Opoku Onyinah (2017). "The Meaning of Discipleship," *International Review of Mission, 106*(2), 216–227.

25 White, *The Desire of Ages*, pp. 136–137 [Kindle Cloud Reader version].

26 Ibid., p. 393.

27 White, The Acts of the Apostles, p. 67.

28 White, Christian Service, Kindle edition, p. 29.

29 Ellen G. White (1897). *The Youth's Instructor*, par. 15.

30 Ellen G. White (1894). Letters and Manuscripts, vol. 9, Ms 105, 1894, par. 20.

31 Ellen G. White (1888). 1888 Materials, p. 991.

CHAPTER 3

1 Onyinah, "*The Meaning of Discipleship,*" p. 242.

2 Ibid.

3 White, Testimonies for the Church, vol. 5, p. 348.

4 White, *The Desire of Ages*, p. 678 [Kindle Cloud Reader version].

5 White, *A Solemn Appeal*, location 292 [Kindle Cloud Reader version].

6 White, *Testimonies for the Church*, vol. 8, location 57884 [Kindle Cloud Reader version].

CHAPTER 4

1 Jeffrey Lynn (2014). Making Disciples of Jesus Christ: Investigating, Identifying and Implementing an Effective Discipleship System, p. 7.

2 Brown, By This They Will Know: Discipleship Principles to Transform the Church, p. 70.

3 White, Christian Service, p. 41 [Kindle Cloud Reader version].

4 White, *The Desire of Ages*, p. 131 [Kindle Cloud Reader version].

5 Whitney, *Spiritual Disciplines for the Christian Life*, p. 14.

6 Ibid., p. 61.

7 White, *Testimonies for the Church*, vol. 5, p. 426 [Kindle Cloud Reader version].

8 Whitney, *Spiritual Disciplines for the Christian Life*, p. 27 [Kindle Cloud Reader version].

9 Brandon Hilgemann (2018). 12 Spiritual Disciplines That Will Make Your Faith Strong.

10 White, The Desire of Ages, p. 59 [Kindle Cloud Reader version].

11 Ibid., p. 57.

12 White, The Desire of Ages, p. 56.

13 White, Testimonies for the Church, vol. 2, pp. 633–634.

14 White, The Desire of Ages, p. 135 [Kindle Cloud Reader version].

15 White, *The Desire of Ages*, p. 61 [Kindle Cloud Reader version].

16 Ellen G. White (1915). *Gospel Workers*. Washington, D.C.: Review and Herald Pub. Assn, p. 316.

17 Ibid.

18 White, *Testimonies for the Church,* vol. 3, location 68066 [Kindle Cloud Reader version].

19 Hilgemann, *12 Spiritual Disciplines That Will Make Your Faith Strong.*

20 White, The Desire of Ages, p. 392 [Kindle Cloud Reader version].

21 White, Testimonies for the Church, vol. 4, p. 374 [Kindle Cloud Reader version].

22 Hull, *The Disciple-Making Pastor*, p. 83 [Kindle Cloud Reader version].

23 Hull, *The Disciple-Making Pastor*, p. 83 [Kindle Cloud Reader version].

24 White, *The Desire of Ages*, p. 362 [Kindle Cloud Reader version].

25 Hull, *The Disciple-Making Pastor*, p. 180 [Kindle Cloud Reader version].

26 White, The Acts of the Apostles, p. 144. [Kindle Cloud Reader version].

27 Whitney, Spiritual Disciplines for the Christian Life, p. 195.

28 Whitney, *Spiritual Disciplines for the Christian Life*, p. 198.

29 White, *Gospel Workers*, p. 37.

30 Ellen G. White (2018). *The Great Controversy*, p. 601 [Kindle Cloud Reader version].

31 Ellen G. White (1896). *Letter 73*.

32 White, *Letter 73*.

33 White, Gospel Workers, p. 236.

34 White, The Desire of Ages, p. 431 [Kindle Cloud Reader version].

35 Ellen G. White (2018). Counsels on Diet and Foods, p. 191 [Kindle Cloud Reader version].

36 Hilgemann, 12 Spiritual Disciplines That Will Make Your Faith Strong.

37 White, Christian Service, p. 150.

38 Whitney, *Spiritual Disciplines for the Christian Life*, p. 115.

39 Ibid. p. 102.

40 Aly Hawkins, David Kinnaman, & Mark Matlock (2019). *Faith for Exiles*. Grand Rapids, Mich.: Baker Books, p. 61.
41 Hilgemann, *12 Spiritual Disciplines That Will Make Your Faith Strong.*

42 White, *Testimonies for the Church*, vol. 6, p. 447.

43 White, *The Desire of Ages*, p. 130 [Kindle Cloud Reader version].
44 White, *The Desire of Ages*, p. 130 [Kindle Cloud Reader version].

45 Ibid., p. 3.

46 White, *Christian Service*, p. 74.
47 Whitney, *Spiritual Disciplines for the Christian Life*, p. 160.

48 Ibid., p. 174.

49 Thomas Haigh, Andrew L. Russell, & William H. Dutton (2015). *Histories of the Internet: Introducing a Special Issue of Information & Culture, 50*(2), 143–159.

50 Jean-Marie Chenou (2014). From Cyber-Libertarianism to Neoliberalism: Internet Exceptionalism, Multi-stakeholderism, and the Institutionalisation of Internet Governance in the 1990s. *Globalizations, 11*(2), 205–223.

51 Rogier Wester & John Koster (2015). The Software behind Moore's Law. *Computer, 46*(10), 66–72.

52 Carmine Gallo (2019). "The Art of Persuasion Hasn't Changed in 2,000 Years," *Harvard Business Review.*

CHAPTER 5

1 Dave E. Cole (2018). *Re-Focus: Creating an Outward-Focused Church Culture,* location 1643 [Kindle Cloud Reader version].

2 Alejandro Bullón (2017). *Total Member Involvement*, p. 23 [Kindle Cloud Reader version].

3 White, *Gospel Workers*, p. 196.

4 White, *Testimonies for the Church*, vol. 4, p. 69.

5 White, *Testimonies for the Church,* vol. 6, p. 296.

6 White, *Christian Service,* p. 12.

7 White, *Christian Service*, p. 49.

8 White, *Testimonies for the Church*, vol. 9, p. 117.

9 Ibid., p. 119.

10 White, *Christian Service*, pp. 124–125.

11 Ibid., p. 41.

12 White, *Testimonies for the Church*, vol. 7, p. 19.

13 White, *Testimonies for the Church*, vol. 9, p. 221.

14 White, *Christian Service*, p. 49.

15 Ibid., p. 44.

16 Ellen G. White, *Prophets and Kings*, p. 263.

17 Hull, *The Complete Book of Discipleship*, pp. 307–308.

18 White, *Christian Service*, p. 62.

19 Hull, *The Disciple-Making Pastor*, p. 16. [Kindle Cloud Reader version].

20 White, *Gospel Workers*, p. 19.

21 Petrie et al. (2016). "Developing a Discipleship Measurement Tool," *Journal of Adventist Mission Studies, 12*(2).

22 White, *Christian Service*, p. 42.

23 Helene Thomas, ed. (2015). *Mentor's Guide: A Companion Resource to the Discipleship Handbook.* Michigan: The Training Center Church Committee of the Michigan Conference of Seventh-day Adventists), location 40 [Kindle Cloud Reader version].

[24] Thomas, *Mentor's Guide,* location 40 [Kindle Cloud Reader version].

[25] Hull, *The Disciple-Making Pastor*, p. 71 [Kindle Cloud Reader version].

[26] Ibid., p. 180.

[27] Hull, *The Disciple-Making Pastor*, p. 168

[28] Ibid., p. 111.

[29] Ibid., p. 179.

[30] White, *Testimonies for the Church,* vol. 9, p. 189.

[31] Lynn, *Making Disciples of Jesus Christ,* p. 48.

[32] Hull, *The Disciple-Making Church*, p. 40. [Kindle Cloud Reader version].

[33] White, *Christian Service*, p. 76.

[34] Bullón, *Total Member Involvement*, p. 22 [Kindle Cloud Reader version].

[35] Bill Hull & Bobby Harrington (2014). *Evangelism or Discipleship*, location 487 [Kindle Cloud Reader version].

[36] White, *Christian Service*, p. 186.

[37] Hull & Harrington, *Evangelism or Discipleship*, location 487 [Kindle Cloud Reader version].

[38] Vanessa M. Seifert (2013). *Discipleship as a Catalyst to Personal Transformation in the Christian Faith*, p. 1.

[39] Ibid.

[40] Hull, *The Disciple-Making Church*, p. 36 [Kindle Cloud Reader version].

[41] Steve Murrell & William Murrell (2016). *The Multiplication Challenge*. Lake Mary: Charisma House, pp. 26–27.

[42] Hull, *The Disciple-Making Church,* p. 45.

[43] Murrell & Murrell, *The Multiplication Challenge*, pp. 26–27.

[44] White, *Christian Service*, p. 21.

[45] White, *The Desire of Ages*, p. 31 [Kindle Cloud Reader version].

[46] White, *Christian Service*, p. 31.

[47] Ibid., p. 206.

[48] Kevin M. Brosius, "Culture and the Church's Discipleship Strategy," *Journal of Ministry & Theology,* 21(1), 123–157.

[49] Bobby Harrington & Jim Putman (2013). *DiscipleShift: Five steps that help your church to make disciples who make disciples*, p. 21 [Kindle Cloud Reader version].

[50] Harrington & Putman, *DiscipleShift*, p. 20.

[51] William F. Cox Jr. & Robert A. Peck (2018). "Christian Education as Discipleship Formation," *Christian Education Journal*, *15*(2), 243–261.

[52] Waylon B. Moore (2013). *The Multiplier: Making Disciple Makers*, location 265 [Kindle Cloud Reader version].

[53] Eldon Babcock (2002). *The Implementation of a Disciple-Making Process in the Local Church*.

[54] White, *Christian Service*, p. 54.

[55] Ibid., p. 55.

[56] Hull, *The Disciple-Making Church*, p. 116.

[57] Robert S. Kaplan & David P. Norton (2006). *Alignment: Using the balanced scorecard to create corporate synergies*. Boston: Harvard Business Review Press.

[58] Kaplan & Norton, *Alignment*.

[59] Ibid.

[60] Ibid.

[61] Ibid.

[62] White, *Christian Service*, p. 54.

CHAPTER 6

[1] White, *Christian Service*, p. 6.

[2] White, *Prophets and Kings*, p. 221.

[3] White, *Christian Service*, p. 62.

[4] Ibid., p. 6.

[5] Ibid., p. 7.

[6] White, *Christian Service*, p. 7.

[7] Ibid., p. 71.

[8] Ibid., p. 6.

[9] Ibid., p. 182.

[10] Harrington, *The Disciple-Maker's Handbook*, p. 172 [Kindle Cloud Reader version].

[11] Bullón, *Total Member Involvement*, p. 9.

[12] White, *Christian Service*, p. 64.

[13] White, *The Desire of Ages*, p. 131 [Kindle Cloud Reader version].

[14] White, *Testimonies for the Church*, vol. 4, pp. 358–359.

[15] White, *Christ's Object Lessons*, pp. 353–354.

[16] White, *Christian Service*, p. 101.

[17] White, *Testimonies for the Church*, vol. 6, p. 423.

[18] White, *Mind, Character, and Personality*, vol. 1, p. 212 [Kindle Cloud Reader version].

[19] Ellen G. White (2020). *Steps to Christ*. Doral: Inter-American Division Publishing, p. 68.

[20] White, *The Desire of Ages*, p. 142 [Kindle Cloud Reader version].

[21] White, *Christian Service*, p. 75.

[22] White, *The Desire of Ages*, p. 135 [Kindle Cloud Reader version].

[23] White, *The Desire of Ages*, p. 126.

[24] Ibid., p. 135.

[25] White, *Testimonies for the Church*, vol. 9, p. 103.

[26] White, *Testimonies for the Church*, vol. 2, p. 151.

[27] White, *Testimonies of the Church*, vol. 2, p. 122.

[28] Ellen G. White (1913). *The General Conference Bulletin* (May 29, 1913), p. 34.

[29] Ellen G. White (2010). *Education*, p. 307 [Kindle Cloud Reader version].

[30] White, *Testimonies of the Church*, vol. 9, p. 140.

[31] Hull, *The Disciple-Making Church*, p. 96.

[32] Hull, *The Disciple-Making Church*, p. 97.

[33] Ibid., p. 70.

[34] Ron Bennett, *Intentional Disciplemaking: Cultivating spiritual maturity in the local church*. Colorado Springs, CO: NavPress, location 153 [Kindle Cloud Reader version].

[35] Onyinah, "The Meaning of Discipleship."

[36] Hull, *The Disciple-Making Church,* p. 37.

[37] White, *Steps to Christ,* p. 46.

[38] White, *Testimonies for the Church,* vol. 6, p. 309.

[39] White, *Testimonies for the Church,* vol. 2, pp. 510–511.

[40] White, *Christ's Object Lessons,* p. 354.

[41] White, *Testimonies for the Church,* vol. 4, p. 145.

[42] White, *Christian Service,* p. 85.

[43] Ibid., p. 183.

[44] White, *The Desire of Ages,* p. 26 [Kindle Cloud Reader version].

[45] White, *Steps to Christ,* p. 83.

CHAPTER 7

[1] Greg McKeown (2014). *Essentialism: The Disciplined Pursuit of Less.* United Kingdom: Random House Group Company, p. 10.

[2] Ibid., p. 70.

[3] All Martin Luther quotes retrieved from https://www.quotetab.com/martin-luther-quotes-about-prayer.

INDEX

Printed in Great Britain
by Amazon

81055855R00119